Love Works
The Essential Couples Therapy Workbook
Ray Vila

Contents

Copyrights		V
Introduction		VI
1.	Chapter 1: Laying the Foundation for Effective Communication	1
	Understanding Your Love Language	
	Self-Reflection Exercise: Discover Your Love Language	
	Active Listening Techniques for Couples	
	Mindful Communication Practices	
	Expressing Needs Without Guilt	
	Needs Inventory Checklist	
	Creating a Safe Space for Vulnerability	
2.	Chapter 2: Overcoming Fear of Vulnerability	12
	Reflection Exercise: Fear Inventory Worksheet	
	Building Trust through Transparency	
	The Importance of Emotional Safety	
	Techniques for Emotional Uncovering	
	Celebrating Vulnerability as Strength	
3.	Chapter 3: Building Emotional Intelligence	25
	Emotional Trigger Reflection Exercise	
	Developing Emotional Resilience	

The Role of Empathy in Relationships
Practicing Emotional Check-ins
Journaling for Self-Reflection

4. Chapter 4: Navigating Conflicts Constructively ... 36
   Conflict Management Checklist
   The Art of Constructive Criticism
   Role-Playing Conflict Scenarios
   Techniques for De-escalating Tensions
   Setting Boundaries with Empathy,

5. Chapter 5 Rekindling Intimacy and Connection ... 48
   Reflection Section: Daily Rituals Checklist
   Exploring Physical Intimacy through Touch
   Rediscovering Shared Interests
   Creating a Romantic Atmosphere at Home
   The Power of Surprise in Relationships

Review Request ... 59

6. Chapter 6 Life Transitions and Relationship Growth ... 61
   Family Mission Statement Exercise
   Career Changes and Relationship Balance
   Embracing New Beginnings Together
   Reflection Exercise: Resilience Through Change

7. Chapter 7 Injecting Excitement into Routine ... 70
   Quick Date Ideas Checklist
   Engaging in New Hobbies Together
   Adventure and Travel for Couples
   Celebrating Milestones Creatively

8. Chapter 8: Prioritizing Time for Each Other ... 80
   Interactive Exercise: Time Audit for Couples

      Establishing Weekly Relationship Check-ins
      Digital Detox for Quality Time
      Scheduling Intimacy and Connection

9. Chapter 9: Celebrating Diversity in Relationships — 90
      Cultural Storytelling Session
      Bridging Personal Value Differences
      Value-Mapping Exercise
      Inclusive Communication Techniques
      Role-Playing Diverse Scenarios
      The Role of Family Traditions
      Retirement Planning for Couples

10. Chapter 10: Long-Term Relationship Growth — 102
      Vision Board Exercise
      Continuous Learning as a Couple
      Revisiting and Refining Relationship Skills
      Building a Legacy of Love
      Celebrating Shared Achievements
      Renewing Commitment through Annual Retreats

Review Request — 114

Conclusion — 116

References — 119

Copyright © 2025 by Ray Vila

All rights reserved.

No portion of "Love Works" may be reproduced in any form without written permission from the publisher or author, except as permitted by U.S. copyright law.

This publication is designed to provide accurate and authoritative information in regard to the subject matter covered. It is sold with the understanding that neither the author nor the publisher is engaged in rendering legal, investment, accounting or other professional services. While the publisher and author have used their best efforts in preparing this book, they make no representations or warranties with respect to the accuracy or completeness of the contents of this book and specifically disclaim any implied warranties of merchantability or fitness for a particular purpose. No warranty may be created or extended by sales representatives or written sales materials. The advice and strategies contained herein may not be suitable for your situation. You should consult with a professional when appropriate. Neither the publisher nor the author shall be liable for any loss of profit or any other commercial damages, including but not limited to special, incidental, consequential, personal, or other damages.

First edition. 2025

Introduction

In a vibrant city, Sam and Alex, a couple much like any other, were ensnared in the monotony of work and family life. Their once-strong connection faded, giving way to frequent arguments and scarce laughter. Feeling trapped and doubtful of their future together, they turned to the strategies outlined in **Love Works**. Gradually, they restored their bond through improved communication and conflict resolution, fostering empathy and understanding. Though not unique, their journey showcases the transformative power of practical tools combined with hope.

This workbook is your guide to achieving a similar transformation. It offers practical strategies and exercises to improve communication, resolve conflicts, and deepen intimacy. Whether you've been together for a few years or several decades, this book provides the tools necessary to nurture a harmonious and long-lasting relationship.

My vision is to provide a transformative guide that offers actionable solutions. This book is designed to inspire and uplift you, showing you that a fulfilling partnership is within reach. As long as there is a desire to overcome what damaged the collaboration and love to forgive, this workbook is the right tool to bring back the missing trust and indispensable intimacy essential to a successful relationship. But even if you are not in a crisis, there are benefits; you need the desire to enhance your connection.

Love Works is for you—adults in long-term relationships who are seeking to improve intimacy and communication. It is also for those who may not have access to therapy but are looking for self-guided solutions. You deserve a relationship that thrives, not just survives.

What sets this workbook apart? Including relatable real-life examples like Sam and Alex makes the lessons hit home. Each chapter includes exercises, ideas, and measurable outcomes that allow you to see and feel your progress. You will find that this is not just another self-help book; it is a practical tool for real change.

Love Works is organized so that each chapter builds upon the previous one. As you progress, you will find exercises and examples that guide you on a journey of relationship improvement. From understanding your partner's love language to resolving deep-seated conflicts, every chapter offers something new and valuable.

I encourage you to engage with the content and apply the strategies to your life. Change is possible, and this workbook is vital to your journey to a more fulfilling partnership. You can transform your relationship into one rich in understanding and joy with commitment and effort.

The key takeaway from this workbook is that enhancing communication, resolving conflicts, and deepening intimacy in long-term relationships is achievable. Techniques like journaling, role-playing, checkings, and vision boards are recommended because they can effectively help heal damaged relationships. By following the practical and actionable strategies outlined here that apply to your situation, you can create a partnership that is both meaningful and lasting.

A Chinese proverb says, "Find joy in the Journey, purpose in the process." As part of life, relationships are constantly changing and need attention. It's a journey that can be challenging but also a joy once the process becomes a natural part of the relationship.

So, let's begin this journey together. Open your mind, embrace the exercises, and watch as your relationship flourishes. After all, **love works** when we work at love.

Chapter 1: Laying the Foundation for Effective Communication

Consider the story of an old couple celebrating their 50th wedding anniversary, where the husband attributes their lasting bond to two factors: patience and never-ceasing communication. This anecdote underscores a profound truth: effective communication is crucial for a relationship's longevity, transcending mere daily conversations. It is the foundation for a robust partnership, essential for navigating life's challenges and deepening awareness and emotional connections. This chapter introduces strategies and insights for strengthening your relationship through purposeful conversation. By exploring ways to improve how you and your partner articulate feelings and thoughts, we provide practical tools to foster understanding and intimacy. Let's explore how we express love and connect with our significant others.

Understanding Your Love Language

Dr. Gary Chapman first introduced the concept of love languages in his book, *The Five Love Languages*. It offers an interesting lens through which we can view our relationships. Imagine your partner speaks French, and you speak Spanish. Although you both attempt to communicate affection, the messages are lost in translation. Love languages are the dialects of the heart, encompassing five distinct expressions: Quality Time, Acts of Service, Receiving Gifts, Physical Touch, and Words of Affirmation. Each language is a unique expression of love, and understanding them can significantly improve how you communicate with your partner. Quality Time is about undivided attention and shared moments, Acts of Service involve doing helpful things for your partner, Receiving Gifts represents thoughtful gestures, Physical Touch includes hugs and kisses, and Words of Affirmation encompass verbal expressions of love. Each language speaks to a different aspect of love, and recognizing which resonates most with your partner is crucial.

By understanding love languages, you can unlock a new level of communication, one where misunderstandings are minimized because you are attuned to how your partner perceives love. Imagine the joy of receiving a gift when what you truly crave is a heartfelt compliment. Tailoring your expressions of affection to align with your partner's love language ensures your efforts are understood, appreciated, and deeply felt. This alignment leads to more transparent communication and a stronger emotional connection, reducing the chances of miscommunication. In principle, speaking your partner's love language is like finding the right radio frequency; suddenly, the static disappears, and the message comes through loud and clear.

To uncover your love languages, consider taking a love language quiz together. This activity can be both enlightening and fun, setting the stage for deeper conversations about what makes each of you feel loved and appreciated. Reflective journaling is another powerful tool. Spend time writing your experiences where you felt most loved and ask your partner to do the same. Compare notes, discuss your findings, and search how these insights can enhance your daily interactions. Acknowledging each other's preferences is the first step toward more meaningful communication.

Self-Reflection Exercise: Discover Your Love Language

Assign time for reflection on instances when you felt deeply valued. Consider whether it was during moments of your partner's undivided attention or a surprise gesture of thoughtfulness. Record these moments and prompt your partner to do likewise. This process will highlight your predominant love language, shedding light on your emotional preferences.

Regularly discussing and adapting to each other's changing love languages is vital. Relationships are dynamic, and what resonated with you last year might not hold the same significance today. Schedule monthly check-ins to talk about your love languages, allowing room for growth and change. This ongoing dialogue ensures that you both remain attuned to each other's emotional needs, fostering a relationship full of understanding and empathy. Incorporating these straightforward yet impactful approaches into your relationship establishes a strong base for effective communication, guaranteeing that love is conveyed most effectively.

Active Listening Techniques for Couples

Active listening is the secret factor to a successful relationship, though it sounds deceptively simple. Imagine your partner is speaking, but instead of thinking about what you'll say next or checking your phone, you're entirely focused on them. That's active listening—giving your full attention without distractions. It's about genuinely hearing your partner, not just the words but the emotions behind them. This kind of listening is a rare gift in a busy world. Reflective listening, a key component, involves paraphrasing what your partner has said, ensuring you've understood correctly. This clarifies any potential confusion and shows your partner that you are invested and their words matter to you. It's a way of saying, "I'm here, and I'm listening."

To enhance your listening skills, consider employing some tried-and-true techniques. Start by paraphrasing your partner's words; this simple act can prevent countless misunderstandings. For example, if your partner mentions feeling overwhelmed with work, you might say, "It sounds like you're stressed about your workload lately." This shows that you're not only listening but also empathizing. Asking clarifying questions is another powerful tool. If something isn't clear, don't hesitate to ask, "Can you tell me more about what's going on at your job?" It's not just an interrogation but a genuine effort to understand. Non-verbal affirmations—like nodding or maintaining eye contact—also play a critical role. They signal your partner that you're engaged and interested, even if you haven't said a word.

However, active listening doesn't come without its trials.

Emotional triggers can make it difficult to keep your cool. Perhaps your partner says something that hits you deeply, and suddenly, your mind is racing instead of listening. Identifying these triggers is the first step toward overcoming them. Take a deep breath and remind yourself that your partner's words are not a personal attack. Pre-existing biases can also cloud your listening skills. Hearing another perspective is tough if you've already decided on a topic. Handle conversations with an open mind, prepared to consider viewpoints that differ from yours. This openness paves the way for healthier and more enriching dialogue.

To practice active listening, engage in activities that build these skills in a fun and supportive environment. Role-playing scenarios can be particularly effective. Pick a common issue—perhaps deciding where to go on vacation—and take turns actively listening to each other's preferences. Focus on paraphrasing and asking questions. Another enjoyable exercise is listening games. Sit back-to-back and take turns describing a scene or object. The listener's job is to recreate the description, relying only on what they've heard. It sounds simple until you realize how much we rely on visual cues! Both activities highlight the importance of clear communication and the hurdles of relying solely on words.

Incorporating any or all of the active listening techniques will fundamentally change your communication dynamic, creating an environment where both partners feel honestly heard and appreciated. This shift encourages discussions that promote understanding over conflict, nurturing the best approach to solving disagreements.

Mindful Communication Practices

Mindful communication, being fully present and intentional in our interactions, is a transformative approach to enhancing daily dialogue. The origin of Mindfulness can be traced thousands of years; it comes from the word sati, which refers to "moment-to-moment awareness" and is a necessary factor of enlightenment in Buddhism. At its core, mindfulness invites us into the present moment, urging us to engage our five senses with our partner with a sincere focus and deliberate speech. Think about a conversation where each word is chosen with care, not just heard but truly listened to, fostering an environment where mutual understanding flourishes. This level of awareness moves beyond mere conversation, letting you connect deeply with your partner's emotions and thoughts. In this sacred space, empathy grows, conflicts wane, and the bonds of your relationship are strengthened. It requires intense effort, but by fomenting present-moment awareness, you ensure that each interaction is meaningful and impactful rather than mechanical or superficial.

The benefits of mindful communication are significant. It curtails emotional reactivity, often the root of heated disputes and misunderstandings. Mindfulness transforms your responses, fostering a space of empathy. It guards against the sharpness of hasty words, encouraging thoughtful, understanding responses. This practice refines communication and elevates the emotional atmosphere of your relationship, leading to a peaceful coexistence. Mindfulness prompts a moment of pause before talking, allowing you to weigh your words and consider your partner's feelings, which promotes a more harmonious interaction.

To integrate mindfulness into your communication, you should start with simple exercises designed to center your mind and body before you begin meaningful discussions. Breathing exercises are particularly effective; taking a few deep breaths before speaking can calm the nerves and clear the mind, allowing for a more focused and intentional exchange. Likewise, mindfulness meditation sessions can help ground you, fostering a sense of inner peace that carries over into your interactions. These practices serve as a bridge to a more mindful way of communicating, setting the stage for meaningful conversations. By tackling each interaction with a calm and open mind, you invite a deeper level of engagement and understanding, paving the way for a more fulfilling relationship.

Integrating mindfulness into your daily interactions need not be a daunting task. Start small, perhaps by incorporating mindful mealtimes, where you both commit to being fully present, savoring the food and each other's company without the distraction of phones or television. This practice converts a routine dinner into a chance for connection and appreciation. Also, please establish evening reflection rituals, where you both take a minute to reflect on the day, sharing thoughts and feelings in a calm and helpful manner. These routines create a rhythm of mindfulness that permeates your days, enhancing your communication and overall relationship.

Mindful communication isn't just a tool; it's a lifestyle choice that can revolutionize how you interact with your partner. By embracing mindfulness, you open the door to a deeper, more meaningful connection, where each word and gesture carries meaning and purpose. This practice invites you to slow down, truly engage with your partner, and appreciate your relationship's nuances. It's about creating a space where love and understanding can flourish, unhindered by the noise and distractions of the outside world. As you continue to integrate these practices into your life, you'll find that communication becomes not just an exchange of words but a profound expression of love and connection.

Expressing Needs Without Guilt

While intimidating, expressing needs in a relationship is crucial for maintaining harmony and satisfaction. Articulating your needs prevents resentment, a silent relationship killer, from building up. It fosters mutual respect as partners gain insight into each other's worlds, promoting understanding and transparency. This, in turn, encourages reciprocation, making both partners feel valued and heard. It's about authenticity in communicating what truly matters to you, not about making demands.

Now, how does one express needs without feeling a pang of guilt or the fear of being perceived as needy? The key lies in assertive communication. Begin using "I" statements, which focus on your feelings rather than pointing fingers. Instead of saying, "You never listen to me," try, "I feel ignored when my thoughts aren't acknowledged." This subtle shift in phrasing reduces defensiveness and keeps the conversation constructive. Avoiding blame language is crucial. Instead of casting aspersions, express how a situation affects you personally. This method encourages openness and collaboration, making it easier for your partner to respond with empathy and understanding. It's about creating a dialogue, not a monologue, where both voices are respected.

Common fears often accompany the act of expressing needs. The fear of rejection can paralyze even the most confident individuals. What if your partner dismisses your needs? This fear is rooted in past experiences where vulnerability was met with indifference or criticism. Overcoming it requires a leap of faith and trust in your partner's willingness to understand. Then there's the fear of conflict. Expressing needs might seem like opening Pandora's box, unleashing disagreements or tension.

However, it's important to remember that healthy conflict can lead to growth and more in-depth understanding. By embracing these fears and addressing them head-on, you create an environment where needs can be expressed freely.

Exercises can significantly assist in overcoming these barriers, transforming need expression into a regular and accepted part of your relationship. Start with a needs inventory checklist. List what you require in various aspects of your life—emotional support, quality time, or even space. Please share this list with your partner, using it as a springboard for discussion. This approach clarifies your needs and invites your partner to reflect on their own. Regular, structured conversations can also help normalize the expression of needs. Consider scheduling a weekly needs discussion, where both partners are encouraged to speak openly about their current desires and challenges. This practice fosters an ongoing dialogue that keeps both partners attuned to each other's evolving needs. Only known needs can be met.

Needs Inventory Checklist

Draft a comprehensive inventory of your fundamental needs, encompassing emotional and practical dimensions. Consider exploring realms such as emotional support, the desire for independence, physical affection, intellectual stimulation, and shared activities. Encourage your partner to undertake the same reflective journey, creating their list of needs. Once it's finished, you can exchange these inventories with a spirit of openness and curiosity. You can use these detailed lists as catalysts for deeper conversations, helping you and your partner through a journey of mutual discovery and understanding. This exercise serves as a bridge to express and comprehend each other's needs without reservation and as a foundation for nurturing empathy, respect, and a profound connection within your relationship.

By weaving these practices into the fabric of your relationship, you cultivate a space where needs are no longer hidden or feared but are part of a healthy, ongoing exchange. Expressing needs becomes a natural extension of your communication, reinforcing the bond between you and your partner. Over time, this openness leads to deeper intimacy and mutual respect, setting the groundwork for a more fulfilling and robust partnership.

Creating a Safe Space for Vulnerability

Embracing vulnerability is crucial for forging deeper connections within a relationship. It involves the courageous act of unveiling one's genuine emotions, fears, and desires without any form of pretense. This level of openness requires a significant amount of courage and trust as it lays the groundwork for a relationship characterized by authenticity and mutual trust. When partners courageously share their vulnerabilities, they embark on a journey of building a bond where trust is not just given but earned and reinforced with each genuine exchange. This process fosters an environment where both individuals can be authentic, free from the masks they wear for the rest of the world. Through this shared vulnerability, partners create a sanctuary of trust—a space where their genuine selves are accepted and celebrated. This foundation of trust and authenticity is essential for a relationship to thrive, as it allows for a deeper understanding and connection between partners, reinforcing the bond and making the partnership more resilient in the face of challenges.

Because actual vulnerability can be so challenging for many people and is indispensable to developing genuine communication in a relationship, the next chapter hammers the difficulties and techniques for overcoming the inherent fears of vulnerability in more detail.

Chapter 2: Overcoming Fear of Vulnerability

Imagine vulnerability as a superhero's cloak, a piece of attire that reveals your hidden strengths and real power while also making you feel exposed. This paradox lies in the fact that many of us hesitate to embrace it despite admiring the courage it takes to wear this cloak. This reluctance stems from facing the fears lurking in our minds' shadows. These fears, while varied, share a common effect: they diminish our willingness to be open and build deep connections with our partners. It runs against our learned, internalized concept of self-preservation. These lies we tell ourselves quietly spread doubts about our worthiness, stir fears of being left behind, and raise concerns about losing our grip on control, leading us to build barriers around ourselves instead of seeking comfort in the connections we desire.

Common fears, like the fear of rejection, often stem from a concern that revealing our true selves will lead to judgment. This fear persuades us that staying guarded is safer than risking the pain of not being accepted. Others grapple with a fear of inadequacy, a persistent belief that they're not enough, which can prevent them from expressing their true desires or needs. The fear of abandonment is another formidable adversary, rooted in a dread of being left alone or unworthy of love. This fear may manifest as clinginess or an aversion to close relationships. Lastly, the fear of losing control can keep individuals from being vulnerable, as it challenges the illusion of self-sufficiency and independence.

Creating a supportive environment for vulnerability goes beyond mere willingness to be open; it demands deliberate actions to cultivate a nurturing atmosphere. Establish discussion ground rules and boundaries to enable expression without fear of judgment or interruption. Embody active compassion and empathy, valuing your partner's feelings and experiences as legitimate, even when they differ from yours. This nurtures further openness, fortifying the cycle of trust and vulnerability. Through persistent effort, such an environment evolves into a sanctuary for both partners, fostering growth and mutual support.

Trust underpins the ability to be vulnerable in a relationship. Without trust, vulnerability becomes a risky endeavor, fraught with the fear of rejection or ridicule. Consistent support and reliability in actions are essential components of trust-building. When your partner knows they can rely on you—whether following through on promises or offering a listening ear—they are more likely to feel secure in sharing their vulnerabilities. Trust is a living entity within a relationship; it requires nurturing and reinforcement through actions that align with words. By demonstrating reliability and support, you signal to your partner that their vulnerability is safe with you, encouraging a deeper connection.

To confront these fears, couples can embark on exercises designed to bring them into the light. A fear inventory worksheet is a helpful tool, inviting you to list and explore your deepest fears. By articulating these fears, you begin to demystify them, robbing them of some of their power. Reflective journaling prompts offer another avenue for exploration. Consider questions like, "What experiences have shaped my fear of vulnerability?" or "How do my fears impact my relationship?" This introspection can lead to revelations that foster empathy and understanding within oneself and between partners. By engaging in these exercises, you initiate the process of recognizing and understanding the barriers that stand in the way of vulnerability.

The origins of these fears often lie in past experiences and societal norms. Childhood experiences, as noted by experts, shape our perceptions of intimacy and trust (*The Counseling Place*). Traumatic events or inconsistent parenting can instill a fear of getting close or relying on others. Cultural expectations also play a role, often dictating that vulnerability is a weakness rather than a strength. Messages from society may suggest that emotional expression is undesirable, especially for certain genders or roles. These ingrained beliefs can create a formidable barrier to vulnerability, but acknowledging their roots is the first step toward overcoming them.

Several strategies can be employed to address and reduce the impact of these fears on your relationship. Cognitive reframing is a powerful method, inviting you to challenge negative thought patterns and reframe them more positively. For example, consider vulnerability an opportunity for growth and connection instead of viewing it as a risk. Positive affirmations can further reinforce this new perspective. Regularly remind yourself of your strengths and the value of your authentic self. Supportive partner dialogues are also essential, offering a space for open communication and mutual support. By sharing your fears with your partner, you invite their empathy and understanding, fortifying your bond and creating a safe space for vulnerability.

Reflection Exercise: Fear Inventory Worksheet

1. **List Your Fears**: Write down the fears that prevent you from being vulnerable.

2. **Explore Origins**: Reflect on past experiences or societal norms that may have contributed to these fears.

3. **Impact on Relationship**: Consider how these fears influence your interactions with your partner.

4. **Strategies for Overcoming**: Identify cognitive reframing techniques, affirmations, or dialogue opportunities to address each fear.

Facing the fear of vulnerability requires courage and commitment, but the rewards are profound. As you begin to unpack your concerns and understand their origins, you pave the way for deeper connection and intimacy. Vulnerability becomes not a source of fear but a powerful tool for authentic engagement, transforming your relationship into a sanctuary of trust and understanding.

Building Trust through Transparency

Openness involves a genuine sharing of thoughts and feelings with your partner, which, in turn, lets both parties glimpse into the very essence of each other's beings. It goes beyond merely admitting faults or disclosing secrets; it entails a daily practice of forthright communication. It's akin to declaring, "Here I am, imperfections and all," and placing trust in your partner's acceptance. By revealing your authentic self, you lay down a solid foundation of trust capable of enduring any challenge. This consistent honesty forms the cornerstone for a deeper mutual understanding, instilling in both partners a sense of security and appreciation.

Transparency is pivotal in building trust, such as clear skies and forecasting good weather. When you're open with your partner, you invite them into your world, creating a shared reality where both of you are on the same page. This mutual understanding fosters deeper trust, as there's no room for hidden agendas or second-guessing each other's intentions. The act of sharing vulnerabilities, those tender parts of ourselves that we often keep hidden, invites your partner to do the same. It's a reciprocal dance of openness that strengthens the relational bond. As you consistently practice truthfulness, you reinforce that your relationship is a safe space for authenticity. This openness paves the way for a resilient and profound connection, where trust is not just an ideal but a lived reality.

Incorporating transparency into daily interactions requires deliberate effort and commitment. Start with regular truth-telling exercises. These can be simple yet impactful, like sharing something that made you anxious or excited during the day. You create a habit of openness by routinely opening up about your internal world. Scheduled transparency talks can further enhance this practice. Please set aside specific times each week to discuss any lingering concerns or feelings, no matter how small. These talks provide a structured environment where honesty is the norm, encouraging both partners to speak freely. Over time, these practices become second nature, fostering an atmosphere of trust and openness.

However, maintaining transparency is not without its challenges. Fear of conflict is a common hurdle, as the truth can sometimes lead to uncomfortable conversations. It's important to remember that conflict, when approached constructively, can lead to growth and understanding. Habitual secrecy, often born from past experiences, can also hinder transparency. These ingrained habits may take time to overcome, but it's possible to break the cycle with patience and persistence. Misaligned expectations between partners can further complicate matters, as differing views on what should be shared can lead to misunderstandings. To navigate these challenges, engage in honest dialogue about what transparency means to each of you. Establishing clear expectations ensures that both partners feel comfortable and respected in their communication.

By embracing transparency, you invite your partner into a deeper, more authentic connection. It's about creating a relationship where both of you feel seen and understood, free from the shadows of doubt or deception. This openness builds trust and enriches your relationship, allowing it to flourish in an environment of mutual respect and understanding. As you continue to practice transparency, you'll find that your relationship becomes a sanctuary of honesty and trust, where both partners can thrive and grow together.

The Importance of Emotional Safety

Envision yourself navigating a tightrope. Below you, there isn't a safety net but an unseen force poised to catch you if you fall. This is the essence of emotional safety within a relationship. It offers you the confidence to be entirely open, showcasing your true self without the dread of judgment or mockery. Emotional safety isn't predicated on unanimous agreement on all matters but hinges on mutual respect and appreciation for each individual's viewpoint. Such acceptance lays the groundwork for a nurturing environment that allows communication to thrive, akin to how plants blossom in a well-cared-for garden. Feeling emotionally secure encourages you to share your aspirations and fears, fostering an intimacy that enriches and reassures both partners.

Creating an emotionally safe space is akin to constructing a cozy nook in your home. It requires attention and care. You can start by practicing listening without interruption. This means genuinely hearing your partner, not just waiting for your turn to speak. It's about giving them your full attention, nodding, and maybe even throwing in the occasional "I see." Validation of feelings is another cornerstone. When your partner expresses an emotion, acknowledge it. You don't need to agree, but recognizing their feelings can make a world of difference. Non-judgmental feedback is also crucial. When offering your thoughts, focus on the issue, not the person. It's the difference between saying, "I noticed the dishes are piling up," versus, "You never do the dishes." This approach fosters a constructive dialogue where both partners feel heard and respected.

The benefits of emotional safety are multiple. When you feel secure in your relationship, trust naturally follows. This trust is the glue that binds partners together, creating a sanctuary where intimacy can thrive. With increased confidence comes reduced anxiety and defensiveness. You're less likely to feel on edge or ready to pounce at the slightest provocation. Instead, you can engage in discussions calmly and open-mindedly, knowing your partner has your back. This environment encourages vulnerability, allowing both partners to share their authentic selves without fear of retribution. As a result, the relationship deepens, evolving into a resilient and fulfilling partnership.

To assess and improve the emotional safety in your relationship, consider engaging in specific exercises designed to strengthen this foundation. An emotional safety assessment can help you identify areas that need attention. Reflect on questions like, "Do I feel comfortable sharing my feelings with my partner?" or "When was the last time we had a meaningful conversation?" These insights can highlight strengths and areas for growth. Safe space agreements are another valuable tool. Sit down with your partner and discuss what each of you needs to feel emotionally secure. These agreements can include commitments to open communication, regular check-ins, or even a "pause" button when discussions become too heated. By crafting these agreements together, you reinforce the idea that emotional safety is a joint effort requiring both partners to be active participants.

As you enhance emotional safety, remember it's an ongoing process, much like maintaining a garden. It requires regular care, attention, and a willingness to adapt. The effort is well worth it, for you'll find the freedom to grow and explore the depths of your relationship in this safe space. Emotional safety becomes the foundation of trust and intimacy, creating a nurturing, supportive, and profoundly connected partnership. Through this lens, vulnerability is not a risk but an opportunity—a chance to engage with your partner authentically and strengthen the bond you share.

Techniques for Emotional Uncovering

Do you ever experience the sensation that your emotions are engaged in an elusive game of hide and seek, skillfully evading your grasp? Emotional uncovering is akin to gently coaxing those hidden feelings out from their concealed nooks and crannies.

It entails the deliberate acknowledgment of those emotions that we habitually, or out of fear, push to the recesses of our minds. This process of deep emotional exploration is pivotal as it fosters a pathway to authentic connection and mutual understanding, both within ourselves and with our partners. By delving into and sharing these deeper emotions, we lay the groundwork for vulnerability, a foundational pillar to building deeper intimacy. This journey of emotional discovery enriches our self-awareness and strengthens the bonds of our relationships, making it an essential endeavor for couples striving for a deeper connection.

Recognizing and sharing these emotions can feel like cracking open a well-sealed vault. Guided emotional inquiries are a helpful starting point. These are targeted questions that encourage you to explore your feelings more deeply. Think of them as gentle prompts nudging you to look inward, asking questions like, "What am I truly feeling right now?" or "What does this reaction reveal about my more in-depth needs?" Visualization exercises can also be effective. Picture the emotions as colors or shapes within you, allowing them to take form and be acknowledged. Sometimes, seeing an emotion visualized helps in understanding its presence and impact. Partner-supported uncovering involves sharing these insights with your partner and inviting them to support you in this exploration. It's like having a trusted companion on a treasure hunt who helps you sift through the emotional landscape with care and curiosity.

Despite the benefits, emotional uncovering comes with its own set of challenges. It's not uncommon to encounter emotional resistance, a natural defense mechanism that kicks in to protect us from perceived threats. This resistance often manifests as an internal wall, blocking the path to vulnerability. Fear of vulnerability itself can be a significant barrier, as opening up can feel like stepping into the unknown without a safety net.

These challenges can make the process daunting, but acknowledging them is the first step in overcoming them. Understanding that these feelings are natural allows you to approach them with compassion rather than judgment.

Supporting each other through emotional uncovering requires patience and empathy. Active listening is crucial—truly hearing your partner without the need to respond or fix things immediately. It's about being present in the moment, offering a safe space for the other to express themselves. Empathy, the ability to put yourself in your partner's shoes, further deepens this connection. Constructive feedback loops also play a vital role. Instead of jumping to conclusions or offering unsolicited advice, provide feedback encouraging further exploration. Ask open-ended questions that invite reflection and understanding. This approach supports emotional uncovering and strengthens the relational bond, fostering a partnership where both feel seen and valued.

Navigating the complexities of emotional uncovering is much like peeling back the layers of an onion—there might be tears, but with each layer, you get closer to the heart of the matter. It's a process that requires courage and trust, both in oneself and in the relationship. By embracing this journey of emotional exploration, you open the door to a more profound understanding of yourself and your partner, creating a foundation for a relationship rich in authenticity and connection.

Celebrating Vulnerability as Strength

Vulnerability is a superpower in disguise, a strength that offers growth and connection rather than weakness. Embracing openness in a relationship is like opening a window to let the fresh air invigorating and refreshing. By allowing yourself to be vulnerable, you release emotional burdens silently weighing you down. This openness may seem daunting, but it brings immense freedom and relief. Vulnerability invites your partner to honestly know you, fostering an environment where trust and intimacy can flourish. It transforms fear into courage, enabling you to connect more deeply. Being vulnerable is not about exposing yourself to criticism but rather inviting understanding and acceptance.

Consider the story of Anna and Brian, who found themselves on the brink of separation. Through therapy, Anna learned to express her feelings of being overwhelmed by caring for everyone but herself, while Brian shared his fears of inadequacy from unemployment. "*Evident Base Therapy Center.*" Their willingness to be vulnerable allowed them to support each other, creating a renewed sense of connection. Famous figures like Brené Brown have also championed vulnerability as a source of strength, demonstrating that embracing our imperfections can lead to profound personal and relational growth. Brown's work highlights how vulnerability fosters empathy and creativity, enabling individuals to live more authentically. These stories remind us that vulnerability is a powerful catalyst for transformation, offering new perspectives on what it means to be strong.

Celebrating vulnerability within your relationship invites you to honor those moments of courage. Consider hosting vulnerability-sharing celebrations, where you and your partner acknowledge times when you've bravely shared your true selves. These celebrations don't need to be elaborate; a simple dinner where you toast to each other's openness can be meaningful. Another idea is to create a ritual of acknowledging courageous moments. Perhaps you exchange notes or small tokens symbolizing appreciation for each other's vulnerability. These gestures reinforce the idea that vulnerability is valued, not feared, in your relationship. Celebrating these moments creates an environment where both partners feel encouraged to be open and honest.

To further practice and honor vulnerability, engage in activities that foster this openness. Keeping a vulnerability journal can be a transformative practice. Dedicate time to jot down moments when you felt vulnerable and how it impacted your relationship. Reflect on the emotions you experienced and the responses from your partner. This exercise deepens your self-awareness and enhances your ability to communicate openly. Partner vulnerability recognition is another valuable practice. Set aside time to share what you appreciate about your partner's vulnerability, highlighting specific instances where their openness strengthened your bond. By recognizing and valuing each other's courage, you reinforce a culture of vulnerability in your relationship.

As you embrace vulnerability as a strength, remember that it's a journey filled with both challenges and rewards. Being vulnerable invites you to step into the unknown with courage and grace, transforming your relationship into a sanctuary of connection and intimacy. By celebrating and practicing vulnerability, you cultivate a resilient, authentic, and profoundly fulfilling partnership. Vulnerability becomes not a risk but a powerful tool for growth, offering new opportunities for understanding and love. This chapter closes with the hope that you will continue to explore the depths of vulnerability, discovering its transformative power in your relationship. As we turn the page, we will delve into emotional intelligence, a key skill to maintain the intimacy that vulnerability brings. Ultimately, the truth is that we all are vulnerable, and without it, there can't be trust.

Vulnerability can bring strong emotions to the surface. Emotional intelligence is critical to deal with them constructively.

Otherwise, opening up and uncovering strong emotions can become messy and lead to fear. Active listening is only possible in an emotionally controlled environment that a high emotional intelligence can provide. The following chapter offers ways to develop this critical skill.

Chapter 3: Building Emotional Intelligence

Think of times when a casual conversation leads to strong emotions, like the mention of your teenage years suddenly unleashing a flood of emotions as swift and potent as a rush of adrenaline. These experiences are known as emotional triggers—a stimulus that sparks a powerful emotional reaction, often rooted in past experiences or deeply ingrained beliefs. These triggers can magically evoke emotions from the depths of our memory, transforming a benign comment into a catalyst for stress, making you question why a simple remark has left you feeling like you've unexpectedly crossed paths with a wild animal.

Emotional triggers have a profound impact on our reactions and behaviors. When triggered, you might experience stress-induced reactions ranging from a racing heart to a sudden urge to flee the scene as if it's on fire. This phenomenon, often called emotional hijacking, occurs when your emotions override rational thought. In these moments, it feels as if your brain has handed the keys to an over-caffeinated raccoon. Understanding these triggers is crucial because they often dictate how we respond to situations and interact with our loved ones. Recognizing them allows us to regain control and respond with intention rather than impulse.

Identifying your emotional triggers requires a bit of detective work. Start by keeping a trigger tracking worksheet, a handy tool where you note down situations that evoke strong emotional responses. Was it a raised eyebrow during a meeting or a particular tone of voice that set off the alarm bells? Reflective questions can also help uncover these triggers. Ask yourself, "What was I feeling right before I reacted?" or "What past experience might this remind me of?" These questions guide you in exploring the root causes of your emotional responses, revealing patterns that might otherwise go unnoticed. By becoming more aware of your triggers, you take the first step toward managing them effectively.

The origins of emotional triggers often lie in past experiences and underlying beliefs. Childhood experiences, for example, can impact how you perceive and react to certain situations. A teacher's criticism in school left you sensitive to feedback, making any critique feel like a personal attack. Memories of Being bullied are a common trigger. Core beliefs and values also play a role. If you've grown up believing that vulnerability is a weakness, you might react defensively when someone points out a flaw. Understanding these origins provides insight into why certain triggers exist, offering a fundamental understanding of yourself and your emotional landscape. It's like peeling back the emotional layers of your personal history, revealing the core beliefs that drive your reactions.

So, how do you manage these triggers effectively? Grounding exercises offer a practical solution. When you feel an emotional hijack coming on, focus on the present moment. Notice five things you can see, four things you can touch, and so on. This exercise helps anchor you in reality, distancing you from the emotional storm brewing inside. Reframing thoughts is another powerful technique. If a comment makes you feel criticized, challenge the negative thought by considering alternative interpretations. Maybe the person was offering genuine advice rather than a critique. This cognitive restructuring shifts your perspective, allowing you to respond with a clearer mind.

Emotional Trigger Reflection Exercise

Take a moment to jot down recent situations that triggered strong emotions. Reflect on these experiences, asking yourself what past events or beliefs might be influencing your reactions. Consider how you might approach similar situations differently in the future, using grounding exercises or reframing thoughts to maintain emotional balance.

Incorporating these strategies into your daily life is like giving your emotional toolkit a much-needed upgrade. Recognizing and managing your emotional triggers lays the foundation for building more substantial emotional intelligence. This awareness benefits your personal growth and enhances your relationships, allowing you to navigate life's challenges with grace and resilience.

Developing Emotional Resilience

Emotional Resilience is the ability to bounce back from adversity and manage stress effectively, like a well-worn tennis ball that always returns to shape, no matter how hard it's hit. This resilience is vital in relationships for maintaining a healthy dynamic, allowing partners to navigate life's inevitable challenges with grace and understanding. Imagine it as a rubber band, flexible yet intense, stretching to accommodate pressures but snapping back to its original form. Emotional resilience ensures that setbacks don't permanently damage the fabric of your relationship, but rather, they become opportunities for growth and deeper connection.

Building emotional resilience is about enduring tough times and actively preparing for them. Stress management techniques can fortify your resilience, acting as a protective shield against life's slings and arrows. Techniques such as deep breathing, meditation, or even a brisk walk can calm the mind and body, reducing stress and restoring equilibrium. Couples might also engage in resilience-building challenges together, like taking on a new hobby that pushes you both out of your comfort zones or tackling a shared goal that requires teamwork and perseverance. These activities strengthen your emotional resilience and reinforce your partnership, showing that together, you can face adversity confidently.

A crucial element in cultivating emotional resilience is adopting a growth mindset. This mindset embraces challenges as opportunities for learning rather than threats to stability. When you view failures as stepping stones to success, you develop a more resilient outlook, ready to face whatever life throws your way. Imagine a couple who, after a heated argument, reflects on what triggered the disagreement and how they could handle it better next time. Instead of letting the argument fester, they use it as a learning moment, strengthening their bond and enhancing their conflict resolution skills. By embracing this growth-oriented perspective, you improve your capacity to adapt, thrive, and maintain a healthy relationship.

Stories of overcoming adversity can inspire and illuminate the path to resilience. Take, for instance, the story of Emily and Jake. They faced the formidable challenge of job loss during a recession. Instead of succumbing to despair, they chose to support each other, viewing the situation as a chance to reassess their priorities and explore new career paths. They navigated financial uncertainty through open communication and shared determination, emerging stronger and more united. Or consider Sarah and Alex, who faced the emotional turmoil of a health crisis. By leaning on each other and seeking external support, they discovered newfound depths of empathy and resilience, turning a potentially devastating situation into a testament to their love and commitment.

Personal anecdotes like these highlight the transformative power of resilience in relationships. They show that while adversity is unavoidable, it doesn't have to define your partnership. Instead, it can become a catalyst for growth and deeper connection. Emotional resilience is not about avoiding challenges but facing them with courage and a willingness to learn. By building resilience, you equip yourself with the tools to weather any storm, ensuring that your relationship remains a source of strength, support, and joy amidst life's unpredictability.

The Role of Empathy in Relationships

High emotional intelligence inevitably leads to empathy. Empathy is the glue that holds the intricate pieces of a relationship together. It's not just about nodding along as your partner shares their day; it's about genuinely feeling what they feel, seeing the world through their eyes. Empathy allows you to connect on a deeper level, fostering a bond that transcends words. It involves emotional attunement, where you tune into your partner's emotions like your heart has Wi-Fi, picking up their signals before they utter a word. This deep connection cultivates a sense of understanding and acceptance, creating a safe space where both partners feel seen and valued. Perspective-taking is another cornerstone of empathy; it involves stepping into your partner's shoes and understanding their world without judgment. This isn't about agreeing with everything they say but recognizing their reality, often leading to more meaningful interactions and deeper connections.

Cultivating empathy doesn't happen overnight; it's like learning to play a musical instrument. You start with the basics and gradually build your skills. Active listening exercises are a great place to start. They require you to give your undivided attention to your partner, listening not just to their words but to the emotions behind them. Try this: focus entirely on what your partner is saying during your following conversation. Don't interrupt or plan your response. Instead, reflect on what you've heard, showing you're genuinely engaged. Empathy mapping is another helpful tool. It involves visualizing and mapping your partner's thoughts, feelings, and experiences. Picture a mind map where you jot down everything you understand about their perspective. This exercise helps you see the bigger picture, fostering greater empathy and understanding.

However, developing empathy can be challenging. Emotional barriers may arise, stemming from past experiences or ingrained beliefs. These barriers act like invisible walls, preventing you from fully connecting with your partner's emotions. Misinterpretations can also pose obstacles. Sometimes, you might misunderstand your partner's feelings or intentions despite your best efforts. It's essential to recognize that these challenges are typical and can be overcome with patience and practice. Start by acknowledging your own emotional barriers and working through them. Engage in open conversations with your partner about any misinterpretations. This dialogue fosters growth and understanding, allowing empathy to flourish.

Practicing empathy requires commitment and effort. Empathy role-plays offer a safe space to explore different perspectives. Choose a scenario, perhaps a recent disagreement, and take turns playing each other's roles. This exercise encourages you to see the situation from your partner's viewpoint, deepening your understanding and connection. Partner perspective exercises are another valuable practice. Share a personal experience during these exercises and invite your partner to reflect on how they perceive it. This activity enhances empathy and strengthens the emotional bond between partners.

Empathy is the heartbeat of a thriving relationship, the silent language that speaks volumes. By cultivating empathy, you nurture a connection rich in understanding and acceptance, creating a resilient and deeply fulfilling partnership. As you continue to explore and practice empathy, you'll find that your relationship becomes a sanctuary where both partners feel genuinely known and cherished.

Practicing Emotional Check-ins

Emotional check-ins are like the relationship version of a routine car maintenance check. They keep everything running smoothly and prevent minor issues from turning into major breakdowns. These check-ins involve regular emotional updates between partners, allowing for open dialogue and a sense of shared understanding. By pausing to assess and acknowledge each other's feelings, you create a space where emotions are shared and understood. It's like meeting with your emotional self regularly, ensuring both partners are on the same page.

In this safe environment, you can discuss anything from daily stressors to deeper emotional concerns while maintaining a healthy relational balance.

Setting a regular schedule is key to conducting effective check-ins. Imagine treating these check-ins like your favorite TV show—something you look forward to each week. Whether it's every Sunday evening or Thursday morning over coffee, choose a time that suits both of you. Consistency helps build a routine, making these check-ins a familiar and comforting part of your relationship. Establishing ground rules beforehand can also enhance these sessions. Agree to listen without interrupting, speak without judgment, and create a space where both partners feel heard. These guidelines ensure that check-ins remain constructive, fostering an atmosphere of mutual respect and trust. Creating a supportive environment encourages open and honest communication, paving the way for deeper connections.

The benefits of regular emotional check-ins extend beyond just catching up on each other's day. They serve as a proactive tool for early conflict resolution, allowing you to address potential issues before they escalate into full-blown arguments. Think of them as a relationship thermometer, helping you gauge the emotional temperature and adjust as needed. Over time, this practice strengthens the bond between partners, creating a resilient and adaptive relationship. Emotional check-ins also reinforce the idea that both partners are invested in maintaining a healthy connection, promoting a sense of partnership and collaboration.

Consider incorporating sample questions and activities to encourage deeper reflection and make these check-ins meaningful. Start with simple inquiries like, "How are you feeling today?" This question invites your partner to share their current emotional state, offering insights into their daily experiences.

Follow up with prompts such as, "What's been on your mind lately?" This encourages a more detailed exploration of thoughts and feelings, allowing both partners to engage in meaningful discussions. Another effective exercise is to reflect on recent experiences together. Could you talk about a shared event or challenge and explore how it impacted both of you emotionally? These activities enhance communication and provide valuable opportunities for empathy and understanding, strengthening the emotional connection between partners.

Emotional Check-In Questions
- How are you feeling today?

- What's been on your mind lately?

- Is there anything you're worried about?

- What has brought you joy recently?

- How can I support you better?

Incorporating these questions into your check-ins transforms them from mere conversations into powerful tools for emotional growth and connection. They encourage both partners to express themselves openly, fostering a relationship that is rich in understanding and empathy. As you continue to practice emotional check-ins, you'll find that they become a cherished ritual, a moment of connection that reinforces your bond and enhances your relationship's overall health.

Journaling for Self-Reflection

Journaling is like having a conversation with yourself, minus the awkward pauses. This technique is a fundamental tool for self-reflection. It offers a relaxing path for emotional growth, which produces clarity in the chaos of life's whirlwind. Putting pen to paper transforms nebulous thoughts and feelings into something tangible and understandable. This process of self-discovery allows you to track emotional patterns, revealing insights that might otherwise remain hidden beneath the surface. Imagine pinpointing why a particular comment irked you or why a specific situation left you feeling elated. As you chart these patterns, you better understand your emotional landscape, equipping yourself with the knowledge to navigate future challenges more effectively.

To enhance this practice, consider using relationship-focused journaling prompts. These prompts encourage reflection on both personal and relational growth. Start with simple questions like, "What am I grateful for in my relationship?" This prompt invites you to focus on the positive aspects of your partnership, fostering a sense of appreciation and contentment. Another powerful prompt is, "How can I support my partner better?" By contemplating this question, you reflect on your role in the relationship and identify areas where you can enhance your partner's experience. These prompts serve as a starting point for deeper introspection, opening the door to meaningful insights that can transform your relationship dynamics.

The benefits of sharing journal insights extend beyond personal growth. When couples openly share their reflections, they create a bridge of mutual understanding. This exchange of thoughts and emotions enhances emotional intimacy, allowing both partners to see the relationship through each other's eyes. Imagine sitting down with your partner and discussing your journal entries. You might discover shared dreams, common concerns, or even hidden fears. This transparency fosters a more profound connection, reinforcing the idea that you're not just two individuals but a united team. By embracing this practice, you create a partnership that thrives on openness and trust, paving the way for a more fulfilling relationship.

To integrate journaling into daily life, consistency is key. You can set up a daily reflection time, a quiet moment to engage in self-reflection without distractions. Whether in the morning with a cup of coffee or before bed, find a time that suits you best. This dedicated space for journaling allows you to process your thoughts and emotions regularly, making it easier to track patterns and insights over time. Consider joint journaling sessions with your partner as well. Set aside a time each week to write together, perhaps focusing on a shared prompt. Afterward, discuss your reflections, exploring the themes and insights that emerged. This practice reinforces the journaling habit and strengthens your emotional connection, creating a shared ritual that enhances your relationship.

Through journaling, you gain a fundamental understanding of yourself and your relationship, transforming abstract emotions into concrete insights. It's a powerful tool for self-discovery, fostering emotional awareness and growth. Integrating this practice into your daily routine lays the groundwork for a rich relationship of understanding and empathy. As you continue to explore this avenue of self-reflection, you'll find that your relationship becomes more resilient and equipped to handle whatever life throws your way.

In this chapter, we've journeyed through the landscape of emotional intelligence, exploring how tools like journaling, empathy, and emotional check-ins can transform your relationship. By embracing these practices, you cultivate a partnership that is both resilient and deeply fulfilling. As we transition to the next chapter, we'll explore how to use these tools to deal with the conflicts daily life inevitably throws on relationships and how, if left unchecked, it can erode the partnership from the inside out. Like a car, attention to detail and constant maintenance are key.

Chapter 4: Navigating Conflicts Constructively

Picture this: two people who share a deep love for each other find themselves amid little disagreements—maybe it's about that toothpaste left uncapped or a laundry basket that seems to overflow every time you turn around. You might also find yourselves clashing over the thermostat temperature or whether the bed is made. Does any of this resonate with your experience? If so, know you're not alone—many couples face similar challenges. Conflicts can feel overwhelming, regardless of their size, but it's important to remember that they are a natural part of even the most substantial relationships. Instead of trying to avoid these situations altogether, the goal is to learn how to navigate through them together. This chapter will help you identify some common triggers of conflict and provide you with supportive strategies to address them. By doing so, we can turn potential arguments into valuable opportunities for growth and more in-depth understanding between you and your partner.

Conflicts can arise from a myriad of situations, but a few common culprits tend to crop up time and again. Financial disagreements, for instance, are a frequent source of tension. Money, whether you have a little or a lot, can be a touchy subject. Financial discussions can often lead to heated debates, whether it's differing spending habits or disagreements over budgeting priorities. Then, there are differences in parenting styles, where one partner might be the disciplinarian while the other is more lenient. These differences can create a divide, leaving both partners feeling frustrated and misunderstood. Lastly, household responsibilities can become a battleground. Who takes out the trash? Who's responsible for cooking dinner? These seemingly mundane tasks can escalate into full-blown disagreements if left unaddressed.

To effectively manage these conflicts, it's crucial for couples to recognize their unique triggers. This requires a bit of self-reflection and open dialogue. Consider keeping a conflict journal, where you can jot down recurring issues and reflect on what might be causing them. This practice helps identify patterns and serves as a starting point for discussions. Regular couple discussions are equally important. Set aside time to talk about what's bothering you without the distractions of daily life. These conversations allow both partners to express their feelings in a safe environment, paving the way for mutual understanding and resolution.

Ignoring these triggers, hoping they will disappear on their own, is a recipe for disaster. Unresolved issues tend to fester, leading to an accumulation of resentment. If left unchecked, this resentment can erode the trust that forms the foundation of any healthy relationship. Over time, minor grievances can snowball into significant issues that become increasingly difficult to resolve. The key is to address these triggers head-on before they have the chance to damage the relationship further.

To prevent these triggers from wreaking havoc, consider developing conflict-prevention plans. Think of these plans as a proactive approach to managing potential disagreements. You reduce the likelihood of conflict by outlining how you'll handle specific situations before they arise. Establishing trigger-response protocols can also be beneficial. These protocols involve setting clear guidelines for responding when a trigger is activated. For example, if financial discussions tend to get heated, agree to take a break and revisit the conversation when both partners are calm and collected. This approach defuses tension and fosters a collaborative environment where both partners feel heard and respected.

Conflict Management Checklist

- **Keep a Conflict Journal**: Document recurring issues and reflect on potential triggers.

- **Schedule Regular Discussions**: Set aside time to address concerns and express feelings.

- **Develop Conflict-Prevention Plans**: Create strategies to manage potential disagreements.

- **Establish Trigger-Response Protocols**: Agree on guidelines for dealing with specific triggers.

Incorporating these strategies into your relationship requires effort and patience, but the payoff is well worth it. Identifying and addressing common triggers creates a more harmonious environment where both partners feel valued and understood. It's about transforming conflict from a destructive force into an opportunity for growth and deeper connection. Remember, every disagreement is a chance to learn more about your partner and strengthen the bond you share.

The Art of Constructive Criticism

Consider the moment you discover the dishes left unwashed in the sink—yet again. That initial wave of annoyance washes over you. Before you let frustration take the lead and escalate the situation, pause and reflect on the power of constructive criticism. It's the bridge between an accusatory "You're such a slob!" and a collaborative "I've noticed the dishes have been left out a few times. This tends to disrupt the kitchen's order. Could we work together on a solution?" Constructive criticism zeroes in on actions rather than character traits. Its goal is to foster improvement and understanding rather than assigning blame. Think of it as performing a gentle but thorough edit on your relationship's narrative—smoothing out the rough patches without discarding the essence of your story together. Constructive criticism encourages personal growth and astute mutual understanding by focusing on specific behaviors and seeking solutions.

Delivering criticism positively can feel like navigating a minefield. Doing it right requires high emotional intelligence and a light touch. But fear not; the "sandwich" method is here to help. It's a tasty approach: start with a positive, layer the critique in the middle, and finish with another positive. For example, "I sincerely appreciate how hard you've been working lately. I think it would help if we shared the chores more evenly. I love how you always make time for us despite your busy schedule."

This method cushions the impact of criticism, making it easier for your partner to digest. Another tip is to offer solutions alongside feedback. Instead of pointing out what went wrong, could you suggest ways to improve? It's like saying, "Here's the map, and I'll walk with you," rather than just pointing out someone's lost. This approach enhances cooperation and strengthens your bond as you work together to find solutions.

However, even with the best intentions, constructive criticism can go awry. Defensive reactions are a common pitfall. No one enjoys hearing they've messed up, even if it's wrapped in a nice sandwich. When faced with criticism, the instinctive response might be to defend or deflect. To counter this, foster an environment where both partners feel safe expressing their thoughts without fear of backlash. Encourage a pause before responding, allowing time to process the feedback calmly. Misinterpretations can also derail constructive criticism. Words can easily be misconstrued, turning constructive advice into perceived attacks. To avoid this, ensure clarity in your communication. Paraphrase what your partner says to confirm understanding, and encourage them to do the same. This practice minimizes misunderstandings and ensures that the intended message is received.

Practicing constructive criticism can be as enlightening as it is challenging. Role-playing scenarios provide a safe space to hone these skills. Imagine a scenario where one partner forgot an important anniversary. Use this opportunity to practice expressing disappointment constructively. Simulated feedback sessions can also be beneficial. Take turns offering feedback on everyday situations, focusing on maintaining a positive and respectful tone. These exercises help build confidence in delivering and receiving criticism, transforming it from a dreaded confrontation into a collaborative conversation. Criticism response drills are another avenue for practice. In these drills, one partner practices receiving feedback without reacting defensively, focusing on understanding the message rather than the delivery.

Embracing constructive criticism can be a game-changer in relationships. It's about creating a space where both partners can grow together, learning from each other's insights and perspectives. By focusing on behaviors and solutions, you foster a resilient and adaptive partnership capable of weathering the storms of life with grace and unity. Constructive criticism isn't just a tool; it's an invitation to deepen your understanding of each other and forge a strong, supportive, and ever-evolving relationship.

Role-Playing Conflict Scenarios

You can create a living space where a couple transforms their living room into a stage, with one partner embodying Shakespeare's eloquence as the other navigates a scheduled dispute as if strategizing in an intricate chess game. This isn't just playful imagination but a strategic role-playing exercise to unravel the complexities of relationship conflicts. Role-playing emerges as a powerful tool for couples, inviting them to momentarily trade places and thereby deepen their empathy and understanding for one another. By simulating potential disagreements in a controlled environment, both individuals gain insights into alternative perspectives and possible reactions, all without the immediate stress of a genuine conflict. This approach refines empathy and also serves as practical preparation for managing real-world disputes, encouraging couples to explore and adopt diverse strategies for resolving conflicts.

I think setting some ground rules is essential to start this enlightening exercise. First and foremost, both partners must agree that this is a judgment-free zone where mistakes are learning opportunities, not points for criticism. Choose realistic scenarios that reflect everyday disagreements—this isn't the time to reenact the finale of a dramatic soap opera. Instead, focus on issues that genuinely affect your relationship, such as disagreements over scheduling or social event planning. For instance, one partner might frequently overcommit to social engagements without consulting the other, leading to feelings of neglect or frustration. Role-play this scenario, with one partner expressing their concerns and the other practicing active listening and response. Choosing scenarios that resonate with your experiences ensures that the practice is relevant and beneficial.

Let's consider a few specific scenarios to role-play. Scheduling disagreements are a common source of tension. Perhaps one partner has a habit of double-booking their weekends, leaving the other feeling sidelined. In this role-play, practice expressing feelings and negotiating a compromise that respects both partners' time and commitments. Another scenario might involve planning a social event where one partner wants a quiet dinner at home while the other dreams of a bustling gathering with friends. Role-playing these situations allows you to explore alternative solutions and find common ground without the pressure of an actual disagreement. Through these exercises, you'll develop a toolkit of strategies for navigating similar real-life conflicts.

The benefits of role-playing extend beyond the immediate resolution of hypothetical conflicts. This practice enhances communication skills, teaching partners to articulate their thoughts and emotions clearly and respectfully. By rehearsing these interactions, couples become more adept at handling actual conflicts with poise and confidence. Role-playing also increases readiness for actual disagreements, as partners have already practiced responding to potential triggers in a controlled environment. This preparedness can lead to more thoughtful and less reactive conversations, reducing the likelihood of escalating tensions. Moreover, role-playing fosters a sense of teamwork and collaboration, reinforcing the idea that both partners are on the same side, working together toward a harmonious relationship.

Role-playing may seem unconventional at first, but it offers a playful yet profound way to improve conflict resolution skills. Couples can gain valuable insights into their dynamics and develop healthier communication patterns by stepping into each other's shoes and navigating hypothetical disagreements. This practice strengthens empathy and understanding and equips partners with the tools needed to handle real-life conflicts with grace and composure. As couples engage in these exercises, they lay the groundwork for a relationship built on mutual respect, trust, and effective communication.

Techniques for De-escalating Tensions

Make a scene where a conversation with your partner suddenly escalates. The volume rises, and the atmosphere becomes charged with emotion. In such moments, de-escalation becomes an invaluable ally, acting as a peacekeeper to prevent the conversation from overflowing with unchecked feelings. The aim here is to sidestep a scenario where emotions become so overwhelming that they cloud the core issue. Mastering the art of de-escalation helps to halt the progression of an argument before it evolves into an irreparable conflict. It's akin to pressing a pause button during moments of heightened intensity, providing a breather for both individuals to regroup and approach the matter with a calmer, more collected mindset. This method is crucial for safeguarding the relationship's integrity, ensuring that disputes are resolved without inflicting enduring harm.

Several strategies can be employed to effectively de-escalate a tense situation. Taking a time-out is one of the most effective techniques. It may sound like something reserved for unruly children, but it's equally beneficial for adults caught in the throes of conflict. Agree on a signal with your partner that indicates when a break is needed. This isn't about running away from the issue but rather stepping back to regain composure. A few minutes apart can work wonders. Utilize deep breathing exercises during this time. Focusing on your breath helps calm the storm within, reducing anxiety and allowing for a more rational response. Another practical approach is creating physical space. Sometimes, the simple act of moving to a different room can provide the distance needed to defuse tension. It allows both partners to collect their thoughts and return to the conversation with a more balanced perspective.

Tone and body language play a pivotal role in how conflicts unfold. A calm tone serves as a soothing balm in heated discussions, signaling to your partner that you're open to resolution rather than escalation. It's not just what you say but how you say it. Lowering your voice can have a powerful effect, encouraging your partner to mirror your composure. Similarly, maintaining an open and non-threatening posture communicates a willingness to engage constructively. Folding arms, clenched fists, or aggressive gestures can unintentionally signal hostility, further stoking the flames of conflict. Instead, focus on an open stance, relaxed shoulders, and gentle eye contact. This body language fosters an environment of safety and respect, paving the way for healthy dialogue.

Practicing de-escalation skills is crucial, and there are exercises designed to build these abilities. De-escalation role-plays offer a safe space to experiment with these techniques. Imagine a scenario where a disagreement over household chores escalates. Practice taking a time-out, using calming language, and employing constructive body language. Reflect on the experience with your partner afterward, discussing what worked and what could be improved. Reflection and feedback sessions are another invaluable exercise. After a conflict has been resolved, take time to reflect individually and then share your insights with each other. Focus on what de-escalation techniques were effective and which ones need refining. This practice not only reinforces learning but also strengthens your ability to manage future conflicts with agility and grace.

Setting Boundaries with Empathy,

Envision a relationship as a thriving garden where freedom and protection coexist through boundaries. These boundaries are not walls but gentle fences, marking personal space and emotional limits to safeguard individuality and mutual respect within the partnership. They guide what behaviors or topics may be sensitive, ensuring the relationship flourishes without overstepping personal well-being.

Establishing these boundaries with empathy involves more than just drawing lines in the sand. It's about engaging in straightforward, honest communication and understanding that everybody needs some personal time. Imagine telling your partner you need some "me-time" without sounding like a rejection. I think expressing this clearly and kindly helps set expectations. It's a dialogue, not a monologue, where both partners communicate their needs and listen to each other. Mutual agreement and respect are the cornerstones of this process. By agreeing on these boundaries together, both parties feel respected and valued, knowing that their comfort and individuality are considered. It's a two-way street that requires patience and understanding.

However, maintaining these boundaries can be as tricky as balancing a spinning plate on a stick. They can be tested by external pressures, like work demands or social obligations, which often push against your set limits. Partners might also test boundaries, sometimes unconsciously, to see if they're flexible. This isn't a sign of disrespect but a natural part of human behavior. Handling these challenges requires vigilance and open communication. When boundaries feel strained, it's time to revisit the conversation. Reinforce why these limits were set and discuss any necessary adjustments. It's a balancing act that requires ongoing attention and care.

Exercises can provide a structured way to practice boundary-setting and ensure they are respected. Consider engaging in boundary negotiation sessions, where you sit down with your partner to discuss and agree on specific boundaries. This isn't about laying down the law but collaborating to ensure both partners feel comfortable and secure. Boundary reflection exercises are also helpful. Could you take time regularly to reflect on whether your boundaries are being respected and if they still align with your needs? Feedback loops for boundary effectiveness can be a game-changer. Periodically check in with each other to discuss how well the boundaries are working and make necessary tweaks. Open dialogue keeps the relationship healthy and adaptive.

As we wrap up this exploration of navigating conflicts, remember that setting boundaries is integral to maintaining a harmonious relationship. It isn't about creating distance but ensuring that both partners have the space to breathe and grow. By forging these boundaries with empathy and mutual respect, you lay the groundwork for a resilient and nurturing partnership. With these tools in hand, you're well-equipped to move forward, ready to explore new dimensions of understanding and connection in your relationship. As we transition to the next chapter, think of boundaries as the supportive framework for the deeper work of building emotional intimacy.

Chapter 5 Rekindling Intimacy and Connection

Envision this scenario: It's an early Tuesday morning, and as you struggle to awake, your mind is already racing with the day's endless tasks. Amid the relentless demands of work, family obligations, and fleeting attempts at maintaining a social life, it becomes alarmingly easy for your relationship to drift into a state of routine neglect. However, the key to reigniting the spark of intimacy often resides in the beauty of everyday rituals. These minor yet consistent habits serve as the adhesive that unites partners, fostering moments of connection within the whirlwind of daily life. Consider these rituals as small but steadfast reminders that reinforce the love and connection you share amidst life's perpetual motion. Remember, making time for intimacy is paramount in any couple's relationship.

You should consider starting your day with a morning gratitude exchange. As you sip your coffee—perhaps the only peaceful moment before the day begins—take a moment to share something you appreciate about each other. It could be as significant as your partner's unwavering support or as simple as their knack for making the perfect cup of coffee. This ritual sets a positive tone for the day, reinforcing the affection and appreciation that form the bedrock of your relationship. In the evening, wind down with reflection talks. As you settle into the quiet of the evening, discuss the day's highs and lows. Sharing these moments foments a more in-depth understanding of each other's experiences and emotions, strengthening your emotional bond.

Specific rituals can further enhance this connection. Make shared morning coffee time a sacred ritual, even if it's just five minutes. This practice ensures you start the day together and creates a shared moment to look forward to. Another idea is to engage in daily "highs and lows" discussions. Each partner takes a turn sharing the best and worst parts of their day, showing insight into their emotional landscape. These discussions lay the groundwork for empathy and support, reinforcing the sense that you're in this together, come rain or shine. It's about creating a rhythm of connection, where each day begins and ends with a nod to your partnership.

Consistency is the key to maintaining this emotional closeness. Like brushing your teeth, these rituals work best when they become a regular part of your routine. Set specific times for them, like during breakfast or before bed, to ensure they don't get lost in daily responsibilities. Integrating these practices into your routine may require some planning, but the effort is well worth it. The regularity of these rituals helps cement their place in your relationship, ensuring each day holds its own moments of connection. These consistent acts evolve relationships from surviving to thriving, fostering a closeness that endures.

Of course, life has a way of throwing curveballs, and maintaining these rituals can sometimes feel like juggling flaming torches while riding a unicycle. Busy schedules and differing priorities often pose challenges. Maybe you're running late for work, or your partner has an early meeting. The key is flexibility. If you can't share your morning coffee, you can send a quick text expressing gratitude. If your evening reflection is interrupted, take a moment to reconnect before sleep. The goal is not perfection but persistence. Find what works for you both and be willing to adapt as necessary, focusing on maintaining your emotional connection despite life's hurdles.

Reflection Section: Daily Rituals Checklist

- **Morning Gratitude Exchange**: Share something you appreciate about each other each morning.

- **Evening Reflection Talks**: Discuss the highs and lows of your day before bed.

- **Shared Morning Coffee Time**: Dedicate a few minutes each morning to connect over coffee.

- **Daily "Highs and Lows" Discussions**: Share your day's best and worst parts to foster empathy and understanding.

Incorporating these daily rituals into your relationship doesn't require grand gestures or elaborate plans. Instead, it's about finding small, meaningful ways to connect daily. These rituals create a tapestry of connection woven from the threads of daily life. They remind you that your relationship is a priority despite the chaos and demands of the outside world. Through these practices, you cultivate a partnership rich in love, understanding, and intimacy, creating a safe harbor amid life's storms.

Exploring Physical Intimacy through Touch

The power of touch in relationships is akin to the secret ingredient in your favorite dish—it binds everything together, making the whole greater than the sum of its parts. Physical touch isn't just a sensory experience; it's a profound form of non-verbal communication that deepens the emotional and physical connections between partners. Think of it as the body's love language. When you hold hands, share a hug, or offer a gentle caress, you're not just making contact; you're speaking with your body. This silent language releases oxytocin, often dubbed the "love hormone," which fosters feelings of closeness and trust. It's like having a built-in relationship glue, and it's all about using it wisely to enhance intimacy.

To deepen your connection, weave massage exchanges into your daily interactions. This practice, far from professional, emphasizes the comforting, intimate act of touch. Simple gestures like a back rub after a taxing day or a foot massage during a cozy TV night convey profound care and attentiveness. Similarly, gentle caressing—be it a reassuring touch on the arm or a tender stroke of the hair—speaks volumes of presence and affection. These acts of kindness foster relaxation and intimacy, nurturing a space where love thrives.

Structured activities can also be invaluable in exploring the depths of physical connection. Hand-holding meditation offers a unique experience. Sit facing each other, hold hands, and breathe together. Feel the warmth and let it anchor you in the moment. This exercise not only soothes but also reinforces the bond between you. Partner yoga sessions are another avenue worth exploring. Yoga is not merely an exercise; it's a journey of synchronicity and balance. As you flow through poses together, you learn to move as one, supporting and depending on each other. It's a beautiful metaphor for partnership, where shared effort leads to harmony and understanding.

However, it's crucial to acknowledge that not everyone experiences touch equally. Comfort levels with physical intimacy can vary widely, influenced by personal history, cultural background, or individual preference. Open discussions about comfort zones are vital. Create a safe space where both partners feel free to express their boundaries and desires without fear of judgment. This dialogue ensures that physical touch remains a source of comfort, not tension. Gradual exploration is also key. Approach new expressions of physical intimacy slowly, respecting each other's pace. This sensitivity reinforces trust and builds a foundation where both partners feel secure in their interactions.

Navigating these different preferences requires patience and empathy. It's about finding a balance that honors both partners' needs. As you explore physical intimacy, remember that it's a collaborative dance. There will be missteps, but these are opportunities for growth and understanding. Communication and trust are key. The goal is not to achieve some ideal state of physical connection but to enjoy the process together, discovering what feels right for both of you. You communicate love and support through touch, nurturing a bond that transcends the spoken word.

Rediscovering Shared Interests

Think of shared interests as the glue that holds the picture frame of your relationship together. They are the activities that bring you closer, creating a mosaic of shared memories and teamwork. Engaging in common interests strengthens your bond, offering opportunities to work as a team and build experiences that are uniquely yours. This collaboration can transform mundane days into adventures, where the sum is indeed greater than its parts. Whether it's a shared appreciation for culinary arts or a mutual love for hiking, these interests cultivate a deeper connection, reinforcing the idea that you are partners in both love and life.

Finding these shared interests might seem like a treasure hunt, but the map is simpler than you think. Start with an interest inventory exercise. Sit down with your partner and list activities you both enjoy or would like to explore. Reflect on past adventures that brought smiles and laughter. Did you once enjoy camping trips or lose track of time painting together? These reflections can reveal forgotten passions waiting to be rekindled. Pay attention to what lights up each other's eyes and consider how these interests can be woven into your current lives. It's about discovering what makes both of you tick and finding avenues to celebrate those interests together.

Once you've identified potential interests, the fun truly begins. Remember, it's about enjoying the process together. Consider diving into cooking classes where you can experiment with flavors and techniques, creating not just meals but memories. If the great outdoors calls your name, embark on outdoor adventures. Whether hiking through scenic trails or kayaking on serene waters, these experiences offer a blend of physical challenge and tranquil beauty. Art and craft projects are another delightful option—a new sport. Engaging in creative pursuits allows you to express yourselves while enjoying each other's company. These activities spark joy and invite you to explore the world—and each other—from new angles, fostering a sense of shared achievement and discovery.

Integrating new interests into your lives can invigorate your relationship, offering fresh perspectives and experiences. Attend workshops together to learn something new. From photography to pottery, workshops provide a structured yet relaxed environment to explore new skills and interests. Joining community groups can also offer a sense of belonging, connecting you with others who share your passions. These groups often host events and activities you can enjoy as a couple, enhancing your social circle and reinforcing your bond. It's about stepping outside your comfort zone and embracing the vast array of possibilities that await together.

The journey of rediscovering shared interests is ever-evolving, adapting as you grow and change. It's not about finding a single interest that defines your relationship but rather continuously exploring and integrating activities that bring joy and connection. Investing time and energy into these shared pursuits creates a rich tapestry of experiences that enhance your relationship's depth and resilience. This ongoing exploration is a testament to your commitment, demonstrating that you value the partnership enough to nurture and celebrate what makes you unique together.

Creating a Romantic Atmosphere at Home

Picture returning home after a long, exhausting day to discover a haven that gently radiates romance. The atmosphere you create plays a vital role in nurturing your connection, transforming ordinary moments into extraordinary experiences. The strategic use of lighting serves as a simple yet powerful tool to foster intimacy. Embrace soft, subdued lighting to create a serene vibe that encourages relaxation and togetherness. Replace harsh, bright lights with the warm glow of table lamps or the enchanting shimmer of fairy lights. This slight adjustment can significantly transform the room's ambiance, providing a tranquil retreat for you and your partner to unwind and reconnect.

Scent and sound are the unsung heroes of romance. A delicate fragrance wafting through the air can evoke memories and emotions, adding an invisible layer of allure to your space. Consider using aromatherapy diffusers with calming scents like lavender or citrus, which can soothe the mind and body. Pair this with a soft music playlist to create an auditory embrace, wrapping you both in melodies that speak to your shared experiences. The gentle hum of a favorite song can transport you to cherished moments, weaving a soundscape of love that enhances your connection.

Every room in your home holds the potential for transformation. The bedroom, often the heart of intimacy, can become even more inviting with thoughtful touches. Add layers of texture with plush throws and soft pillows, creating a cocoon of comfort. Consider a gentle color palette of pastels or earth tones to promote tranquility. In the living room, swap everyday clutter for cozy elements like candles and a snug rug. These changes, though small, can turn an ordinary space into an intimate retreat where conversations flow and laughter lingers.

Integrating romance into daily life doesn't require monumental effort. You can set aside weekly romantic evenings dedicated to each other. Whether it's a candlelit dinner or a movie night under a blanket fort, these evenings offer a chance to escape the routine and focus solely on your partnership. Seasonal decor changes can also keep the romance alive. Embrace the seasons by incorporating elements that reflect the time of year, like fresh flowers in spring or warm, rich hues in autumn. These visual cues keep your environment fresh and inviting, signaling a shared appreciation for the present moment.

Creating a romantic atmosphere is more than aesthetics; it invites deepening your connection. It's about crafting a space that nurtures and celebrates your bond, where every corner whispers of shared love and cherished moments. As you transform your home into a romantic haven, remember that it's the little things—the gentle glow of a candle, the soft strains of a song, the scent of a favorite fragrance—that weave the tapestry of intimacy. These elements come together to create an environment where love can thrive, turning your home into a sanctuary of connection and warmth.

The Power of Surprise in Relationships

Waking up on a regular Saturday morning, only to be whisked away on a spontaneous weekend adventure by your partner, or perhaps finding a heartfelt note tucked into your workbag, turning an ordinary day into something special. These are the moments that surprise brings into a relationship. Surprises have an uncanny ability to invigorate relationships, injecting a dose of excitement and spontaneity that can break the monotony of routine. They remind us that love is a comfortable habit and an ever-evolving adventure filled with unexpected joys. By introducing the element of surprise, you invite a sense of wonder and anticipation, rekindling the spark that sometimes gets dimmed by everyday life.

Surprises don't have to be grand gestures that break the bank or require months of planning. Simple, thoughtful surprises can have a profound impact. Consider planning a surprise date night. It could be as simple as preparing a favorite meal or setting up a cozy movie night with all the trimmings, complete with popcorn and a blanket fort. These small acts of thoughtfulness show your partner that you care and are thinking of them, even amid a busy week. Unexpected love notes are another delightful way to surprise your partner. A quick "I love you" scribbled on a post-it note found in a jacket pocket can brighten their day and reinforce the emotional connection between you.

For those feeling adventurous, spontaneous weekend getaways can offer a refreshing escape from the daily grind. Whether it's a trip to a nearby town or a night spent camping under the stars, these experiences create lasting memories and strengthen the bond between partners. The key is the element of surprise—being whisked away on an unplanned adventure can reignite the excitement and romance that brought you together in the first place. These moments of spontaneity break the routine and remind you both of the joy and fun in your relationship, reinforcing the idea that life together is an exciting journey.

Surprises come with psychological benefits that extend beyond the initial thrill. They boost mood and satisfaction, enhancing overall happiness in the relationship. The unexpected nature of a surprise can lift spirits and provide a much-needed break from the predictability of daily life. Additionally, surprises create lasting memories. The thrill of the unexpected etches these moments into your mind, forming a bank of cherished memories you can look back on together. These shared experiences contribute to a strong emotional foundation, reminding you both of the love and joy underpinning your partnership.

However, there's an art to executing surprises successfully. It's crucial to ensure that the surprise is enjoyable for both partners. Consider your partner's preferences and comfort zones. Not everyone enjoys being the center of attention or being caught off guard. A surprise should be a source of joy, not anxiety. Avoid overwhelming surprises that may cause stress or discomfort. Instead, focus on thoughtful gestures that align with your partner's interests and personality. By tailoring surprises to suit your partner, you ensure the experience is positive and enriching, reinforcing your love and connection.

Chapter 5 has explored how to infuse your relationship with intimacy and connection, from creating a romantic atmosphere to embracing the power of surprise. These elements breathe new life into your partnership, reminding you both of the love that brought you together. Entire chapters are dedicated to these themes to understand their utility better. As we move forward, we'll explore the challenges of navigating life's transitions as a team.

Review Request

Unlock the Power of Connection

"Love is a verb, not a noun." - Ricardo Arjona.

When you give without expecting anything back, you bring more happiness into the world. Together, we can create that ripple effect of kindness and connection.

Would you help someone just like you—someone curious about LOVE WORKS but unsure if it's right for them?

My mission with LOVE WORKS is simple: to help couples grow closer, communicate better, and rediscover the joy in their relationships. But I can't do it alone.

Here's where you come in.

Most people decide on books by reading reviews. Your words can make a big difference. By leaving a review for LOVE WORKS, you can guide someone who needs help finding tools to improve their relationship.

It costs nothing and takes less than a minute, and it could be the spark that saves someone's connection. Imagine your review being the reason a couple learns to communicate better, finds hope again, or feels more love than ever before.

……one more couple builds a stronger bond. ……one more family grows happier. ……one more person figures out the love they've been longing for.

Want to make that kind of difference?

Just scan the QR code below or visit this link to leave your review:

https://www.amazon.com/review/review-your-purchases /?asin=B0DWL1HJG6

If you love helping others, then you're my kind of person. Thank you for sharing your experience and making an impact.

From my heart to yours,

Ray Vila

Chapter 6 Life Transitions and Relationship Growth

Bringing your newborn home marks the beginning of a new chapter filled with both wonder and complexity. It signals a profound shift in your relationship, altering daily life and the core dynamics between you and your partner. Roles and duties that once felt defined and stable now enter a state of flux, introducing you to new challenges and deepening your connection. Adding a child weaves a new layer into the fabric of your relationship, calling for adaptability and steadfast dedication. This chapter is dedicated to guiding you through these significant adjustments, turning potential obstacles into avenues for mutual growth.

Parenthood, with all its joys and challenges, significantly alters the landscape of a relationship. The transition from a couple to a family unit can feel like shifting from a tandem bicycle to a tricycle—suddenly, an extra wheel needs attention. As new parents, you may find yourselves juggling roles and responsibilities that were once clearly defined. Now, they blend into a kaleidoscope of tasks, from midnight feedings to diaper changes. Altered priorities become the norm, with your schedule revolving around nap times and pediatrician appointments. You may see a drop in relationship happiness, as reported by 67% of couples, due to these newfound pressures and the mental health challenges that can accompany them. The need to adapt is paramount, as maintaining the balance between partner and parent becomes your daily mission.

To effectively co-parent, it's essential to engage in shared parenting duties. Think of it as a well-choreographed dance, where each partner knows their steps but is also attuned to the other's rhythm. Sharing obligations ensures that neither of you feels overwhelmed or isolated. Regular family meetings can serve as a touchstone, a moment to recuperate and discuss everything from your child's needs to your own. These meetings foster open communication, allowing both partners to voice concerns, offer support, and plan ahead. It's about creating a cohesive unit where partners are equally invested in the family's welfare. This cooperative approach strengthens your bond and provides a stable environment for your child.

Yet, amidst the wonderful chaos of parenting, it's crucial to maintain your identity as a couple. Scheduled date nights become a lifeline, a chance to reconnect and remember why you embarked on this adventure together in the first place. Whether it's a quiet dinner at home or a night out, these moments are precious opportunities to nurture your relationship. Couple-only retreats offer a more extended escape, allowing both of you to recharge and reflect away from the demands of daily life. These retreats don't have to be extravagant; even a weekend getaway can provide the space needed to focus on each other. By prioritizing time together, you reinforce the foundation of your partnership, ensuring it remains strong and resilient.

Strengthening teamwork in parenting can be achieved through engaging activities designed to foster cooperation and understanding. Co-parenting workshops provide valuable insights and strategies for navigating the intricacies of parenthood. These workshops offer a platform to learn from experts and other parents, sharing experiences and solutions in a supportive environment. Creating a family mission statement is another powerful exercise. This statement serves as a guiding light, encapsulating the values and goals you aspire to uphold as a family. It's a collaborative effort that invites both partners to contribute, ensuring that your shared vision is aligned and that you're on the same page as you navigate parenthood together.

Family Mission Statement Exercise

Take time to sit down together and discuss the core values and goals you want to uphold as a family. What principles do you want to instill in your children? How do you envision your family's future? Write down your thoughts and create a mission statement that reflects your shared vision. Display it where you can see it regularly, reminding you of your commitment to each other and your family.

Parenthood is a transformative journey that can either strengthen or strain a relationship. By embracing the changes and challenges it brings, you and your partner can grow together, forging a robust and nurturing bond. It's about balancing being a parent and a partner, ensuring that both roles are fulfilled with love and dedication. As you adapt to this new chapter in your lives, remember that you're not alone—countless parents have walked this path before, and with the right strategies, you too can thrive amidst the beautiful chaos of parenthood.

Career Changes and Relationship Balance

Embarking on a new career path, brimming with possibilities for the journey ahead, it's always exciting. Yet, as the initial thrill wanes, a maze of challenges emerges. This shift in your professional life mirrors the experience of relocating to a new dwelling—initial excitement gives way to the intricacies of adjustment. These transitions impact not just your individual routine but also the dynamic of your partnership. A surge in stress levels amplified demands on your time, and the need to juggle fresh responsibilities can disrupt the harmony between you and your partner. Navigating extended work hours, a strenuous commute, or adapting to changes in financial status demands open, deliberate dialogue and meticulous planning to preserve a foundation of support and security for both partners.

Navigating career shifts alongside relationship dynamics requires a nuanced approach. Effective time management is key, enabling you to dedicate attention to both your career advancements and your partner. Determining specific time blocks for work and personal life while preserving boundaries ensures professional responsibilities don't overshadow your relationship. Implementing a shared calendar that outlines both work and personal commitments can facilitate understanding and help carve out quality time together. This strategy emphasizes the importance of deliberately prioritizing your relationship amidst career growth.

Open communication is the lifeline that keeps you both afloat during these transitions. Scheduled career discussions offer a platform to openly discuss how these changes impact your relationship. Please set aside regular time to talk about everything from work stress to how your new position affects your time together. Transparent decision-making is crucial, ensuring that both partners feel involved and informed. Whether accepting a new job offer or planning for a relocation, safeguard that both voices are heard. This approach promotes a sense of partnership, reinforcing the idea that you're in this together, navigating the waves of change side by side. You create an environment where both partners feel valued and respected, bolstering your connection even in the face of uncertainty.

Supporting each other's career growth is not just about cheering from the sidelines but actively engaging in each other's professional journeys. Celebrate career achievements, no matter how big or small, with the gusto of a child at a birthday party. Whether getting a promotion or surviving the first week in a new role, these milestones deserve acknowledgment. Celebrating together reinforces your partner's accomplishments and strengthens your emotional bond. Attending career-related events as a couple can further solidify this support. Whether it's a networking event or a company function, showing up together demonstrates that you're invested in each other's success. These events provide opportunities to meet colleagues and understand your partner's work environment, offering insights that can deepen your understanding and appreciation of their professional life.

Partner-led career brainstorming sessions can be a fun and productive way to support each other's ambitions. Set aside time to discuss career goals, brainstorm ideas, and explore potential opportunities. This collaborative approach reworks career planning into a shared adventure, where both partners contribute their insights and support. It's about being each other's sounding board, offering encouragement and constructive feedback. These meetings foster a sense of teamwork and ensure that both partners feel supported in their professional pursuits. By actively engaging in each other's career growth, you create a partnership that thrives on mutual respect and shared aspirations.

Navigating career changes while maintaining relationship balance is a challenge that requires effort, patience, and a touch of humor. It's about finding harmony between personal aspirations and the needs of your partnership, ensuring that both elements coexist rather than compete. As you adapt to these transitions, remember that you're not alone—many couples have faced similar challenges and emerged stronger on the other side. With acceptable time management, open communication, and mutual support, you can navigate this chapter of your lives with confidence and gracefully, ensuring your career and relationship flourish.

Embracing New Beginnings Together

New beginnings are to relationships what spring is to nature—a fresh start brimming with possibilities for growth. They represent those pivotal moments when you pack up the past, sometimes literally, as you move to a new home or adjust to shifts in family dynamics. Whether you're relocating to a new city or welcoming a new family member, these changes offer a unique opportunity to reinvent and strengthen your relationship. Rather than viewing these transitions as disruptions, consider them invitations to explore your partnership's new facets. These fresh starts encourage you to face the unknown together, armed with the knowledge that every challenge is a chance to evolve and deepen your connection.

Preparing for these changes involves more than just logistics; it requires a mindset of optimism and collaboration. Creating a vision board is a practical first step. Gather magazines, scissors, and glue, and start dreaming. Visualize your future together by cutting out images, words, and symbols that resonate with your shared goals and aspirations. This creative exercise helps clarify what you both want and serves as a tangible reminder of your collective dreams hanging proudly in your home. It's an engaging way to align your visions and keep your eyes on the prize, even when the path gets rocky.

Goal-setting workshops are another effective tool. Please go ahead and dedicate an afternoon to sit down with your partner and outline specific objectives you'd like to accomplish together. These could range from financial goals, like saving for a dream vacation, to personal ones, such as learning a new skill together. By setting clear, achievable goals, you create a roadmap that guides you through the intricacies of new beginnings. This process encourages clarity and accountability, ensuring that both partners support each other's aspirations. It's about building a future where both of you feel seen and valued, with goals that reflect individual desires and the shared vision for your relationship.

Flexibility and adaptability are crucial when navigating the uncharted waters of new beginnings. The ability to practice open-mindedness can transform potential stressors into opportunities for growth. Life is unpredictable, and the best-laid plans often need adjusting. Embracing uncertainty with a spirit of curiosity rather than fear allows you to face challenges with resilience. Remember that adaptation isn't about abandoning your plans but refining them in response to changing circumstances. It's like a dance, where sometimes you lead, and sometimes you follow, always moving, agreeing with your partner. You create a dynamic relationship that can weather any storm by staying open to change.

Building resilience through change is about surviving transitions and thriving within them. Resilience-building activities can help fortify your relationship against the inevitable ups and downs. Consider engaging in activities that challenge you both physically and mentally, like hiking a new trail or taking a dance class together. These experiences foster teamwork and trust, reinforcing your ability to navigate challenges together. Reflecting on past successes is another powerful exercise. Take time to reminisce about previous hurdles you've overcome as a couple. What strategies did you use? How did those experiences strengthen your bond? Drawing on these memories reminds you of your capacity to conquer adversity and emerge stronger.

Reflection Exercise: Resilience Through Change

Dedicate a peaceful evening to intimately discuss the transitions you've navigated together as a couple. Begin by acknowledging the successes and pinpointing moments of strength and unity that led to positive outcomes. Then, shift focus to areas where there is room for improvement, analyzing challenges that may have momentarily hindered your progress. Reflect deeply on how these experiences have sculpted the contours of your relationship, enhancing your understanding and bond. Carefully document these reflections, creating a tangible record of your journey. This process celebrates your resilience and equips you with a personalized blueprint for facing future changes with confidence. By embracing this reflective practice, you affirm your collective ability to surmount any obstacle, reinforcing the foundation of your partnership with each shared insight.

As we wrap up this chapter on embracing new beginnings, remember that each transition is an opportunity to renew your relationship and redefine what it means to be a team. By embracing change with optimism and adaptability, you build a partnership that is not only resilient but also deeply fulfilling. New beginnings are not just about starting over but about starting anew, enriched by the lessons of the past and the promise of the future. As you move forward, carry with you the knowledge that together, you can navigate any change, turning each new beginning into a stepping stone toward a stronger, more vibrant relationship.

In the following section, we will elaborate on innovative strategies and ideas for infusing your relationship with joy and levity, exploring the pivotal role shared laughter and fun play in sustaining a deep, meaningful connection.

Chapter 7 Injecting Excitement into Routine

Contemplate moments when life with your partner feels like a series of predictable routines: breakfast, work, dinner, repeat. The vibrant spontaneity that once electrified your days together seems to have faded into the background, overshadowed by the monotony of daily life. However, this is not a cause for concern. The spirit of spontaneity hasn't vanished; it's simply lying dormant, ready to be reawakened and embraced once again in your shared existence. Think of spontaneity as that vital spark that injects your relationship with moments of unexpected delight and excitement, counterbalancing the routine. It's what transforms an ordinary day into an exhilarating adventure together. Inviting spontaneity back into your lives opens the door to a deeper emotional connection, where every unplanned moment can evolve into a treasured memory. It's about welcoming the unpredictable, reigniting the flame of curiosity and exploration, and rejoicing in the happiness of simply being together.

Planning spontaneous date nights might sound like an oxymoron. After all, how do you plan spontaneity? However, a little preparation can go a long way in making those last-minute outings possible. Start by creating a list of quick date ideas. Jot down activities that are easy to organize and don't require a Ph.D. in logistics. Whether it's a late-night ice cream run or a sunset walk in the park, having a go-to list makes seizing the moment a breeze. Another clever idea is preparing a "date night jar" filled with activity suggestions. Write down various ideas on slips of paper and pull one out the next time you're in need of an impromptu adventure. It's like spinning a wheel of fun, where every choice leads to a new experience. This jar becomes a treasure trove of possibilities, ready to transform any ordinary evening into an extraordinary one.

Now comes the fun part: diving into creative and easy-to-plan ideas. Picture this: an impromptu stargazing session. Grab a blanket, head to your backyard or a nearby park, and gaze up at the night sky. Let the stars be your backdrop for whispered dreams and shared laughter. Or how about a last-minute picnic in the park? Pack some snacks and drinks, and head out to enjoy nature's dining room. The simplicity of it all is refreshing, reminding you both that romance doesn't require extravagance. You can go to the new ice cream place in town. A visit to a local art gallery or museum is another delightful option. Wander through the exhibits, hand in hand, and let the art inspire conversations that transcend the everyday. These activities require minimal preparation but offer maximum impact, turning ordinary moments into cherished memories.

Of course, spontaneity has its challenges, but they're not insurmountable. Busy schedules can often feel like the villain in your romantic narrative, swooping in to thwart your plans. But flexibility is your secret weapon. Look for pockets of free time, even if they're just an hour or two, and use them to indulge in spontaneous outings. Remember that it's not about the quantity of time but the quality of the connection. Differing interests can also pose a challenge. Maybe you're an art enthusiast, and your partner prefers the great outdoors. The key is compromise. Alternate between activities that cater to each other's inclinations, ensuring that both partners feel valued and included. It's a dance of give and take, where the goal is to enjoy each other's company, whatever the activity.

Quick Date Ideas Checklist

- **Impromptu Stargazing Session**: Grab a blanket and head to an open space to enjoy the night sky.
- **Last-Minute Picnic in the Park**: Pack some snacks and drinks, and find a cozy spot in your local park.
- **Visit a Local Art Gallery or Museum**: Explore exhibits and let the art spark conversations.

The beauty of spontaneity lies in its ability to surprise and delight, reigniting the spark that drew you together in the first place. It's about breaking free from the constraints of routine and inviting adventure into your relationship. Whether it's a spontaneous date night or a simple change in plans, these moments remind you of the joy and excitement of being together. Embrace the unexpected and let spontaneity be your guide, transforming the ordinary into the extraordinary.

Engaging in New Hobbies Together

Think of your relationship as a fun blank canvas, where each moment you share adds brightness and color to your ever-evolving masterpiece. Trying out new hobbies together adds vibrant strokes to this canvas, making your connection even richer. These shared activities are like a spark that brings excitement to your partnership, giving you both the chance to learn, laugh, and grow together. This adventure strengthens your bond and reveals delightful new sides of each other, deepening your respect and affection. Diving into new interests transforms everyday routines into a thrilling array of possibilities, with each experience offering a unique way to weave new layers into the beautiful tapestry of your relationship.

Choosing a hobby can be as exciting as selecting a destination for a spontaneous road trip. It starts with a simple conversation. Talk about things you've always wanted to try or skills you wish to hone. This dialogue sparks ideas and highlights your individual interests, laying the groundwork for finding common ground. Exploring local community classes is a fantastic way to dip your toes into new waters. From pottery and painting to culinary arts and music lessons, these classes offer structured environments where you can learn at your own pace. They also provide a shared experience, fostering a sense of teamwork as you navigate new challenges together. The joy of learning something new, with a sprinkle of humor from inevitable missteps, creates unforgettable memories.

Once you're ready to dive into a new hobby, consider a variety of options that cater to both your interests. Pottery or painting classes can be enriching, allowing you to express creativity while enjoying each other's company. Imagine the satisfaction of creating something tangible together, whether it's a quirky mug or a colorful abstract painting. Gardening and plant care offers another avenue for exploration. Tending to a garden requires patience and cooperation, which strengthen any relationship. Watching your plants blossom under your care is akin to watching your relationship bloom, each new leaf a testament to your collaborative efforts. Learning a new language is yet another option, providing a playful challenge that encourages communication and teamwork. Visualize practicing phrases and laughing at mispronunciations while forging a more profound connection through shared learning. Dancing lessons, whether it's salsa or ballroom, add a physical dimension to your hobbies. They require coordination and cooperation, turning each dance into a celebration of your partnership.

Embracing hobbies together is about weaving consistency into the fabric of your relationship. Mark your calendars for regular hobby sessions, treating these moments as non-negotiable dates that enrich your bond. This deliberate scheduling ensures your shared interests thrive, undiminished by the whirlwind of daily responsibilities. Revel in the joy of small victories, from mastering a new dance move to nurturing a plant to full bloom. These triumphs, no matter their size, chart your journey of shared discovery and growth, amplifying the joy of your collective achievements. Remember, celebrating these milestones need not be elaborate; sometimes, a shared glance or a clink of glasses is all it takes to honor your journey together.

Incorporating new hobbies into your daily life is like planting seeds in a garden. With time, patience, and care, they grow into strong, vibrant connections that enrich your relationship. These shared activities offer a respite from the pressures of daily life, providing a space where you can unwind and enjoy each other's presence. They remind you there is always room for laughter, learning, and love amidst the chaos and routines. So go ahead, pick up that paintbrush, plant that seed, or lace up those dancing shoes. Every new hobby is an adventure waiting to unfold, and each discovery is a new chapter in the story of your relationship.

Adventure and Travel for Couples

Standing at the edge of adventure, the thrill of the unknown beckons. Think of it not as a leap off a cliff but as a metaphorical jump into shared experiences that transform the mundane into the magnificent. Adventure binds couples closer, weaving their experiences into a rich tapestry of memories more vivid than any photograph. It tests and stretches boundaries, fostering trust and revealing hidden strengths and vulnerabilities. Together, navigating the unexpected, couples strengthen their bond, making every heartbeat a testament to their growth and reinforcing the foundation of their partnership.

Planning adventurous experiences requires a bit of finesse, akin to orchestrating a symphony where both partners' desires harmonize. Start by researching destinations together, transforming the planning phase into an adventure in itself. Whether poring over maps or scrolling through travel blogs, this collaborative effort ensures that the adventure caters to both partners' interests. Discuss what excites you—be it the tranquility of the mountains or the vibrant chaos of a bustling city. Set adventure goals that encapsulate your shared desires. Perhaps it's conquering a challenging hiking trail or immersing yourselves in a new culture. These goals offer a sense of direction, turning daydreams into tangible plans. Remember to keep an open mind and be ready to adapt. Flexibility is key when embarking on adventures, allowing you to embrace the unexpected with enthusiasm rather than apprehension.

The world is your playground, offering a myriad of adventures to suit every taste and risk level. Camping or hiking trips invite you to reconnect with nature and each other, far from the distractions of daily life. Picture yourselves navigating forest trails, the only sounds being your laughter and the rustle of leaves. These trips offer a chance to unplug, focus on the essentials, and appreciate the simple joys of companionship. Weekend city getaways provide a different flavor of adventure. Explore new environments, indulge in local cuisines, and soak up the vibrant culture of a bustling metropolis or a town's local barbecue festival. The thrill of discovering hidden gems and sharing new experiences revitalizes your connection, infusing it with fresh energy. Trying extreme sports like rock climbing can be a game-changer for those craving a bit more adrenaline. Scaling heights or navigating rugged terrains requires teamwork and trust, transforming fear into triumph. Finally, exploring cultural festivals immerses you in the rich tapestry of global traditions. From colorful parades to culinary delights, these festivals offer a feast for the senses, inviting you to celebrate diversity and unity.

Travel, in its essence, is a passport to growth. It exposes you to diverse cultures and perspectives, broadening your horizons and enriching your relationship. As you encounter new customs and traditions, you gain insight into your partner's worldview, fostering empathy and understanding. Shared problem-solving during travels often presents opportunities to strengthen your partnership. Whether deciphering a foreign language or navigating a lively market, these challenges demand collaboration and creativity. Each hurdle overcome together becomes a testament to your resilience and adaptability. Traveling invites you to step out of your comfort zone and embrace the strange with open arms. It's a reminder that growth often rests beyond the boundaries of routine, waiting to be discovered.

In the grand tapestry of life, adventure and travel are the vibrant threads that weave excitement and novelty into your relationship. They invite you to explore the world and each other, discovering new facets of your partnership with every journey undertaken. Adventure is not just an escape but a return—to each other, to the essence of what makes your relationship unique. So pack your bags, grab your partner's hand, and set forth into the world, where every corner holds the promise of discovery and every path leads to a deeper connection.

Celebrating Milestones Creatively

In the tapestry of life, milestones are the colorful patches that highlight growth and achievement. They mark moments when two people pause to acknowledge where they are and how far they've come. Celebrating these milestones is more than just an excuse for cake and balloons; it's about reinforcing commitment and joy, serving as a testament to the shared journey. Whether it's an anniversary, a significant personal achievement, or just surviving the week without losing your keys, these moments are worth celebrating. They remind you of the bond you've built and your shared dreams, strengthening emotional connections with each commemoration.

Creative celebrations breathe life into these milestones, turning them into lasting memories. Consider creating a personalized scrapbook or memory box. Fill it with photos, mementos, and love notes that capture the essence of your relationship. Each page or item becomes a chapter in your shared story, a tangible reminder of the moments that matter most. When you look back, you don't just see pictures; you see the laughter, the challenges, and the triumphs that define your partnership. Hosting a themed celebration at home is another delightful way to honor these occasions. Whether it's a retro 80s night or a cozy pajama party, choose a theme that resonates with your shared interests and history. These gatherings don't have to be extravagant; the thought and effort make them unique. A themed celebration transforms an ordinary evening into an extraordinary event filled with laughter and connection.

Milestones also offer a unique opportunity for reflection and planning. Write letters to each other for future reading. Capture your thoughts, dreams, and hopes for the future, then tuck them away to be opened later. These letters become time capsules of your relationship, revealing how much you've grown both individually and as a couple. Setting new relationship goals during these moments of reflection can also be incredibly rewarding. Please discuss what you hope to achieve together, whether it's traveling to a new destination, learning a new skill, or simply spending more quality time. These goals provide a roadmap for the future, safeguarding that your relationship continues to evolve and blossom.

Involving family and friends in milestone celebrations adds another layer of joy and community. Virtual celebration ideas are perfect for those who can't be physically present. Host a virtual party where loved ones can join from anywhere in the world, sharing your happiness and offering blessings. Technology bridges the distance, allowing everyone to be part of the celebration. Community potluck gatherings are another way to include those you cherish. Invite friends and family to bring a dish, creating a feast that reflects the diverse tapestry of your relationships. It's a celebration of love, friendship, and the bonds that hold us together. For those who prefer a more adventurous celebration, consider organizing a group adventure experience. Whether it's a hike, a day at the beach, or a themed escape room challenge, these activities create shared memories and reinforce the connections that make life meaningful.

As you celebrate these milestones, remember that it's not just about the event but the meaning behind it. These celebrations reflect your relationship, a testament to the love and commitment that have brought you to this point. They are opportunities to pause, reflect, and plan for the future, ensuring your relationship continues growing and flourishing. Whether surrounded by family and friends or enjoying a silent moment together, these milestones remind you of your journey and the adventures yet to come. Embrace these moments, celebrate with imagination and joy, and let them be a beacon in your relationship, guiding you toward a future bursting with love and connection.

As we wrap up this chapter on injecting excitement into routine, remember that variety is the spice of life, and your relationship deserves a sprinkle of it now and then. Do as many as you can or think you need. Just choose what looks good to you and go. These activities and celebrations draw you closer, reminding you of your vibrant, living partnership. In the next chapter, we will explore the importance of prioritizing time for each other amidst life's demands, ensuring that your relationship remains a top priority in your busy lives. This is the first step to making the relationship a close one.

Chapter 8: Prioritizing Time for Each Other

Jane and Tom are trying to find moments for each other amid their busy lives. Jane has a demanding job, while Tom balances household responsibilities with his career, which means their time together is often brief, like fleeting glimpses of an eclipse. The relentless pace of daily life can overshadow the importance of nurturing their connection. Yet, in relationships, time acts as a precious currency—investing. It wisely yields rich dividends. Mastering time management is crucial for making both partners feel cherished, vital, and connected. It's more than finding moments for quick conversations or occasional dates; it involves deliberately creating openings to strengthen their bond and enhance their joy together.

Balancing work and personal life is a task that often feels like spinning plates. On the one hand, you have career aspirations demanding your attention, and on the other, personal pursuits that bring happiness and fulfillment. Add the relationship component, and it can feel like a juggling act worthy of a circus. But here's a little secret: balance doesn't mean equal parts; instead, it means finding harmony in allocated time. Allocating time for individual pursuits is equally important as these activities provide personal growth and satisfaction, which, in turn, benefits the relationship. When partners support each other in pursuing their interests, they foster an environment of mutual respect and understanding. This balance ensures that neither partner feels overshadowed or neglected, preventing the feeling of one partner being a mere footnote in the other's life.

To tackle the time management challenge, please use some practical techniques that make this task less daunting. Shared calendars are a game-changer. By scheduling commitments, events, and even downtime, couples can avoid the dreaded double-booking conundrum. Prioritizing tasks together is another strategy that can convert chaos into calm. Sit down at the start of the week and map out what needs to be done, identifying tasks that require immediate attention versus those that can wait. Doing this together creates a shared agreement of each other's priorities and responsibilities, furthering teamwork and collaboration. This approach streamlines daily activities and ensures that both partners feel their time is respected and valued.

In our tech-savvy world, there's no shortage of tools designed to aid in time management. Time-blocking apps can be invaluable for organizing your day into manageable segments. These apps allow you to allocate specific time slots for work, leisure, and relationship activities, ensuring nothing falls through the cracks. Shared digital planners offer a centralized hub for tracking appointments, commitments, and even spontaneous plans. These tools help couples stay on the same page, reducing the likelihood of miscommunication and forgotten plans. Utilizing these resources can transform time management from a dreaded chore into a seamless and efficient process.

Despite our best intentions, time management doesn't come without its challenges. Setting boundaries with work commitments is a common hurdle. It's all too easy to let work seep into personal time, especially in a time where remote work blurs the line between office and home. Establishing clear boundaries is essential. Communicate with your employer about after-hours availability and set specific times when work emails and calls are off-limits. This approach protects personal time and ensures the relationship doesn't fall victim to professional demands. Another challenge is preventing over-commitment to social obligations. While having a bustling social calendar is terrific, it can leave little room for quality time with your partner. Learn to say no to non-essential events, prioritizing those that truly matter and leaving time for your relationship to thrive.

Interactive Exercise: Time Audit for Couples

Conduct a time audit together. Track how you spend your time for one week, noting activities and the hours dedicated to each. Compare your findings and identify areas where you can adjust to create more quality time. Discuss what activities can be minimized or eliminated and where you might incorporate joint activities or leisure. This exercise provides insight into your time usage and highlights opportunities for improvement.

By embracing these time management strategies, you create a foundation where your relationship can thrive amidst the demands of modern life. It's about making conscious choices that prioritize your partnership, ensuring it remains a central and cherished part of your daily existence. As you navigate time management challenges, remember that the goal is not perfection but progress. Minor adjustments can lead to significant improvements, creating an environment where both partners feel valued, respected, and, above all, loved.

Establishing Weekly Relationship Check-ins

In the whirlwind of a typical week, brimming with meetings, errands, and the unforeseen, it's all too common for relationships to be nudged to the sidelines, overshadowed by the pressing demands of daily life. Herein lies the transformative power of weekly relationship check-ins, a practice akin to finding an eye in the storm. Moment of calm to reflect, reconnect, and realign with one another. These check-ins act as essential pit stops amid life's race, offering a structured moment for heartfelt communication and mutual reflection. They're an opportunity to pause and appreciate the journey together, celebrate the successes, and thoughtfully navigate areas needing attention. This practice ensures that lines of communication remain open, preventing minor misunderstandings from escalating into significant obstacles.

Setting a consistent time and place is essential to make these check-ins productive. You can choose a time when both of you will likely be relaxed, not rushing off to the following commitment. Perhaps you can set intentions for the week ahead on Sunday evening when the weekend's hustle has calmed. The setting should be comfortable and free from distractions—your cozy living room or a favorite café could serve as the perfect backdrop. Prepare topics for discussion once you've settled on a time and place. Think of it as a mini-agenda that ensures you cover both the heights and lows.

Sample questions can guide your dialogue and make the process feel natural rather than forced. Start with a simple "What went well this week?" This opens the floor for positivity and gratitude, setting a warm tone. Follow up with "What could we have done differently?" to introduce any challenges or concerns gently. "How can I support you better?" invites constructive feedback and reinforces the idea that you're both on the same team, striving to support and uplift each other. These questions are not meant to be rigid but guideposts that help keep the conversation on track, ensuring it remains meaningful and constructive.

The benefits of consistent check-ins are manifold. They provide an early warning system for potential issues, allowing you to address them before they escalate. Think of it as catching a small leak before it becomes a flood. This proactive approach can prevent misunderstandings, resentment, and emotional distance from creeping into the relationship. Moreover, regular check-ins reinforce mutual goals. Through discussing both personal and shared aspirations, you ensure that your paths remain aligned, strengthening the partnership with every conversation. It's like adjusting a ship's sails to keep it on course, even when the winds of life shift unexpectedly.

Integrating weekly check-ins into your routine fosters a culture of openness and trust. It's about creating a safe space where both partners feel heard, valued, and understood. This practice transforms communication from a reactive necessity to a proactive choice, prioritizing the health and happiness of your relationship. In this space, you can explore emotions, share dreams, and navigate challenges together, fortifying the connection that binds you. Check-ins become a cherished ritual, a moment each week when the outside world fades and the focus shifts entirely to nurturing the bond you share.

Digital Detox for Quality Time

In today's digital age, smartphones and screens often act as unwelcome intruders in relationships, turning deep conversations into brief, distracted exchanges. This constant barrage of notifications and digital demands can sideline meaningful connection, making partners feel more like cohabitants than companions. Ironically, the very tools designed to connect us can foster a sense of disconnection, placing an invisible wedge between partners. This phenomenon of being ever-present online yet absent at the moment undermines the intimacy and understanding crucial to a strong relationship, leaving an emotional void.

To combat this digital drift, consider implementing a digital detox—a strategy as refreshing as a cool breeze on a hot day. Start by establishing tech-free zones in your home. The bedroom is a prime candidate; keeping it screen-free transforms it into a sanctuary for rest and reconnection. Extend this principle to other areas, like the dining table, where conversations can flourish without the interrupting buzzing phone. Setting specific "no-screen" hours can also be beneficial. Designate times throughout the day, perhaps during meals or an hour before bed—when screens are off-limits. This creates pockets of undistracted time when you and your partner can focus solely on each other. These steps may initially feel like going cold turkey from a tech addiction, but the benefits far outweigh the temporary discomfort.

The question arises once devices are removed: what should we do with this newfound time? This is where creativity and spontaneity take center stage. Outdoor walks or bike rides offer a chance to explore your surroundings while engaging in conversation free from digital distractions. The fresh air and change of scenery can invigorate both body and mind, setting the stage for a deeper connection. Alternatively, dust off those board games or puzzles lurking in the closet. These activities encourage teamwork, laughter, and a bit of friendly competition, rekindling the playful spirit that daily routines might have overshadowed. Cooking meals together can also be a delightful way to spend quality time. Whether you're trying a new recipe or perfecting a beloved dish, the process of creating something together fosters collaboration and communication. Plus, the reward is a delicious meal to share.

The benefits of reducing screen time extend beyond just filling the hours. Minimizing digital distractions improves focus and attention, making each moment with your partner more meaningful and memorable. Conversations become deeper and more engaging as neither partner is tempted to sneak a glance at their phone mid-sentence. This heightened presence enhances the emotional connection, allowing partners to hear and understand each other honestly. Without the constant buzz of notifications, you create a space where intimacy can flourish, unencumbered by the digital noise that often drowns out heartfelt exchanges.

Moreover, a digital detox can act as a reset button for your relationship, reminding you of the simple joys of being together. It's about rediscovering the art of conversation, the warmth of a shared smile, and the comfort of knowing that, in this moment, there's nowhere else you'd rather be. It reinforces the idea that while technology can offer convenience and connection, nothing compares to the richness of actual, uninterrupted time with your partner. As you embrace this practice, you'll likely find that the relationship feels more vibrant and alive, infused with the energy that comes from genuine engagement. The digital world can wait; your relationship deserves the focus and attention only a mindful presence can provide.

Scheduling Intimacy and Connection

In the whirlwind of daily obligations, intimacy, and connection can often feel like distant memories, like that yoga class you keep promising to attend. Yet, intentionally scheduling time for intimacy is not just a romantic notion; it's a necessity. Ensuring you allocate time for these moments prevents your relationship from slipping into the shadows of neglect. It's like watering a plant—not enough attention, and it wilts. Regularly dedicating time to connect reinforces emotional bonds and reminds you that your relationship remains a sanctuary amidst the chaos. This intentionality doesn't have to be grand or elaborate. Sometimes, the simplest gestures yield the most profound connection.

Practical strategies for scheduling intimate moments can transform this concept into a reality. Start with regular date nights. These aren't just for the early days of courtship; they're even more crucial as relationships mature. Whether it's a night out on the town or a cozy evening at home, date nights create a dedicated space for reconnection. Planning weekend getaways can also work wonders. A change of scenery offers a break from routine and a chance to focus solely on each other, even if it's just a short drive away. These getaways need not be extravagant; think of them as mini-vacations for your relationship. By setting these dates in stone, you commit to prioritizing your partnership, reminding each other that your relationship is worth the investment of time and energy.

To keep things lively and engaging, consider a variety of intimate activities. At-home spa nights, for instance, can be both relaxing and romantic. Set the mood with soft music, scented candles, and perhaps a glass of wine. Take turns pampering each other with massages or soaking in a warm bath together. Creative art sessions are another unique way to connect. Whether painting, sculpting, or crafting, engaging in creative pursuits can be both fun and revealing. You might discover new talents or simply enjoy creating something together. Dance lessons add an element of playfulness and physical closeness. Whether mastering the tango or just swaying in your living room, dancing fosters a physical connection that words often can't express. These activities infuse your relationship with variety and excitement, ensuring that intimacy remains a vibrant and cherished part of your lives.

Despite the best-laid plans, life has a knack for throwing curveballs. Managing unforeseen obligations can be one of the biggest hurdles in maintaining your schedule. Flexibility becomes key. Instead of viewing a disrupted plan as a failure, see it as an opportunity to adapt. If a work meeting runs late and derails your date night, consider a late-night dessert run or even a morning coffee date the next day. Adapting plans as needed ensures that while the details might change, the intention behind them remains constant. It's not about sticking rigidly to a schedule but about consistently making space for each other, even if it means getting creative with your time together.

The importance of scheduling intimacy and connection cannot be overstated. It's a conscious choice to prioritize your relationship in a world filled with distractions and demands. By taking deliberate steps to carve out time for each other, you reinforce the foundation of your partnership, ensuring it remains strong and resilient. These moments, big or small, remind you of the love and commitment you share, fortifying your bond against the ebbs and flows of life. As you continue to nurture this connection, you'll find that these intentional acts of intimacy enhance your relationship and enrich your personal well-being.

In summary, this chapter has explored various strategies to

ensure partners prioritize their time together despite the fast pace of modern life. From managing daily schedules to intentionally setting aside intimate moments, each approach is designed to deepen the connection and enrich the partnership. Moving forward, the next chapter will deal with the significance of embracing and celebrating diversity within relationships, highlighting how it can enhance and add layers of complexity and beauty to the journey shared by couples.

Chapter 9: Celebrating Diversity in Relationships

Culture encompasses shared values, norms, and practices that are deeply rooted in geography, history, language, and even religion. These elements influence behavior, communication styles, and expectations. For example, in some cultures, family involvement is deeply ingrained, while individual autonomy is prioritized in others. Recognizing these differences is crucial for navigating relationships and avoiding unintentional misunderstandings.

Your partner's cultural background can reveal much about their habits and perspectives. Have you ever wondered why your partner insists on celebrating certain holidays with gusto or why they seem reserved during discussions? Cultural norms and historical influences often hold the answers. In high-context cultures, for example, communication may rely more on nonverbal cues and implicit understanding, whereas those from low-context backgrounds might prefer direct and clear conversations. Understanding these nuances can prevent misunderstandings and boost empathy. By exploring each other's cultural stories, you gain insights into behaviors and values, fostering a more harmonious relationship.

To deepen this understanding, consider engaging in cultural storytelling sessions. Sit down with your partner and share your cultural histories, perhaps over tea or during a quiet evening. Discuss family traditions, significant events, and the values you grew up with. Sharing family heritage through photos and artifacts can be a powerful way to connect. Imagine flipping through old photo albums or watching home videos, each image sparking stories and laughter. These sessions aren't just about recounting facts; they're an opportunity to see the world through your partner's eyes, forming a link of understanding and respect.

Cultural awareness is like adding a splash of color to a grayscale painting. It increases cultural sensitivity, expands your perspective, and allows you to appreciate the richness of diversity. As you learn about each other's backgrounds, you become more attuned to the subtleties of your partner's experiences and emotions. This heightened awareness promotes empathy, enabling you to respond with understanding rather than judgment. By embracing cultural diversity, you open the door to a deeper connection, one that celebrates differences rather than fearing them. It's about creating a space where both partners feel valued and understood, fostering a relationship that thrives on mutual respect.

To actively discover each other's cultures, try cooking traditional dishes together. Not only is it a delicious way to learn, but it also transforms the kitchen into a classroom of sorts. Picture yourself preparing a meal from your partner's culture, savoring the flavors and aromas that tell stories of their heritage. Attending cultural festivals is another fantastic way to immerse yourself in each other's traditions. Whether it's dancing at a local fiesta or sampling exotic food, these experiences offer a window into the vibrancy of your partner's culture. Watching documentaries on cultural history can further enhance your understanding, providing context and depth to the stories your partner shares.

Cultural Storytelling Session

Set aside an evening to share stories of your cultural heritage. Use photos, artifacts, or music to spark conversation. Discuss family traditions and significant events that have shaped your values. This exercise deepens your understanding of each other's backgrounds and strengthens your bond through shared storytelling.

By actively engaging with each other's cultural backgrounds, you enrich your relationship and create a foundation of empathy and understanding. It's about celebrating the diversity that each of you brings to the table, weaving a tapestry of love that honors both individuality and togetherness. As you explore these elements, you'll find that your relationship is not just a partnership of two individuals but a beautiful blend of cultures and experiences, each contributing to a vibrant and dynamic whole.

Bridging Personal Value Differences

It's important to understand that the preferences for minimalism and tidiness versus an eclectic, "lived-in" atmosphere reflect the core values that guide our everyday decisions and interactions within the relationship. Initially, this difference may lead to playful teasing in a shared living space where one partner values minimalism while the other prefers a more relaxed vibe. These core values are a guiding star, subtly yet significantly steering our behaviors and decisions. They influence everything from lifestyle choices to how we communicate and resolve conflicts. For example, a person who values independence may prioritize solo activities, while someone who holds community and connectedness dear might seek constant interaction. Understanding these core beliefs is crucial because they affect how we navigate our shared lives.

Now, discussing differing values can sometimes feel like trying to defuse a bomb with a toothpick. The key is to engage in open and respectful dialogue. Start with value-mapping exercises, where you and your partner list and share your most important values. This exercise not only highlights differences but also uncovers common ground. Establishing discussion guidelines ensures that conversations remain constructive. Agree to listen actively, suspend judgment, and avoid interrupting. Creating a safe dialogue space allows partners to express their values without fear of dismissal or ridicule. This openness fosters understanding and paves the way for mutual respect.

Embracing different values can be like opening a window to growth, letting in fresh air and new perspectives. When you explore each other's values, you embark on a personal and relational development journey. These differences offer opportunities for learning, where you can step into your partner's shoes and view the world from their vantage point. This perspective shift enhances problem-solving skills as you learn to approach challenges using diverse tools. Rather than seeing differing values as obstacles, view them as stepping stones to a richer, more nuanced relationship. This mindset transforms potential conflicts into avenues for collaboration and innovation.

To align values while respecting individuality, engage in exercises designed to find common ground. Creating a shared values chart is a practical way to visualize overlapping values. You could list your top values and see which ones align. This chart is a testament to your shared beliefs and a reminder of the values holding your relationship together. Identifying overlapping values reinforces the idea that, despite your differences, you share a foundation of typical principles. This exercise also highlights areas where compromise may be necessary, encouraging both partners to negotiate and find solutions that honor individual beliefs while supporting the partnership.

Value-Mapping Exercise

Take time to individually list your top ten personal values. Share these lists with each other, discussing what each value means and why it holds significance. Use this exercise to identify shared values and explore how they can be integrated into your relationship.

Through these practices, you cultivate a relationship that celebrates diversity in values. It's about creating a partnership where both voices are heard and respected, fostering a sense of unity without erasing individuality. As you navigate the landscape of personal values, remember that it's not about changing each other but about growing together and finding harmony in the beautiful symphony of your differences.

Inclusive Communication Techniques

Make each exchange between you and your partner a carefully aimed throw, with every word selected for its ability to connect accurately and thoughtfully. Inclusive communication is the art of crafting these exchanges to be mindful and respectful, valuing the vast array of experiences each partner contributes to the relationship. This approach involves consciously avoiding assumptions, stereotypes, and generalizations that could unintentionally cause hurt. Instead, it focuses on using language that celebrates each individual's unique background, ensuring that differences are not merely acknowledged but genuinely respected. This level of consideration and awareness is the cornerstone of building a relationship grounded in mutual understanding and trust.

Creating an inclusive dialogue is akin to setting a table for a feast where everyone feels welcome and valued. Active listening with empathy is a vital ingredient. It involves giving your full attention, not just hearing but truly understanding your partner's words and emotions. This practice fosters an environment where both partners feel heard and respected. Asking open-ended questions can also enrich your conversations. Instead of a simple "Did you like the movie?" try "What did you think of it, and how did it make you feel?" These questions encourage deeper dialogue, inviting your partner to share their thoughts and feelings without restraint. This openness paves the way for a more profound connection, where both partners feel valued and understood.

However, achieving inclusivity in communication is not without its challenges. Unconscious biases can creep in, like uninvited guests at a dinner party, influencing how we perceive and respond to our partner's words. These biases are often deeply ingrained, shaped by years of societal conditioning. Overcoming them requires a conscious effort to question and reframe our assumptions. Language barriers can also pose obstacles, especially in relationships where partners speak different native languages. Miscommunications can arise, leading to frustration and misunderstandings. Navigating these barriers demands patience and a commitment to finding common ground, often involving a mix of verbal and non-verbal cues to ensure clarity and comprehension.

To hone your inclusive communication skills, engage in practical exercises designed to enhance understanding and empathy. Role-playing diverse scenarios can be particularly enlightening. Imagine a situation where you and your partner disagree on a cultural tradition or practice. You gain insight into your partner's worldview nuances by stepping into each other's shoes and articulating your perspectives. Language sensitivity workshops can also be beneficial. These workshops provide a safe space to explore and practice inclusive language, offering communication tools and techniques across cultural and linguistic divides. These exercises build confidence and proficiency, transforming potential points of conflict into opportunities for growth and connection.

Role-Playing Diverse Scenarios

Choose a cultural or social topic where you and your partner may have differing views. Take turns expressing each other's perspectives, focusing on understanding rather than defending your position. After the exercise, discuss insights gained and how they might influence your future conversations. This practice enhances empathy and deepens your appreciation for your partner's unique experiences.

By actively engaging in these practices, you create a relationship environment where inclusivity is an aspiration and a lived experience. It's about crafting a dialogue where both partners feel valued and respected, regardless of their differences. Through inclusive communication, you build a partnership that celebrates diversity, fostering a connection that is not only resilient but also rich in understanding and love.

The Role of Family Traditions

Family Traditions are the invisible threads weaving through our lives, shaping who we are and how we relate to others. These traditions, handed down through generations, carry the weight of cultural heritage and the comfort of familiarity. They provide a sense of belonging and continuity, reminding us of our origins. In relationships, these traditions influence dynamics by imparting shared values and expectations. For instance, if one partner grew up celebrating the winter holidays with grand family gatherings. At the same time, the other experienced quieter, intimate celebrations; these differing backgrounds can affect how they envision their own holiday traditions. Understanding and respecting these differences is key to fostering harmony and connection.

Integrating diverse family traditions into a relationship can be as enriching as it is challenging. It requires a delicate balance of honoring each partner's customs while creating new ones. A blended holiday celebration might incorporate elements from both partners' backgrounds, allowing for a rich tapestry of traditions reflecting their unique partnership. Whether combining a traditional family dish with a new recipe or blending holiday customs, these efforts signify respect and appreciation for each other's heritage. Honoring each partner's family customs doesn't mean sacrificing one's own traditions; instead, it's about finding common ground and creating a shared experience that encapsulates both worlds.

Embracing family traditions offers numerous benefits, particularly in strengthening bonds and creating shared memories. Traditions provide a sense of unity and continuity, offering comfort and stability amidst life's uncertainties. They serve as anchors, reminding partners of the shared values and experiences that bind them together. Creating new traditions together is equally important. It allows couples to carve out their identity, establishing rituals reflecting their values and aspirations. Whether it's starting a new tradition of an annual family retreat or a simple weekly ritual, these shared activities foster a deeper connection, reinforcing the idea that the couple is building a life and legacy together.

Couples might join annual family tradition brainstorming sessions to celebrate and create traditions. Set aside time each year to talk about and evaluate the traditions that hold meaning for both partners. This exercise can involve reflecting on past traditions and brainstorming new ones that align with the couple's evolving interests and values. Documenting traditions in a family book is another meaningful activity. This book can serve as a repository of cherished memories, capturing the essence of each tradition through stories, photos, and reflections. It's a tangible reminder of the couple's journey and the legacy they are creating. Hosting tradition-sharing gatherings can also be an excellent way to celebrate existing traditions and introduce new ones. Invite family and friends to participate in these gatherings, sharing stories and experiences and highlighting the richness of diverse traditions.

Family traditions, whether inherited or newly created, hold the power to deepen connections and enrich relationships. They provide a framework for celebrating the past while embracing the future, offering couples a unique opportunity to blend their histories into a shared narrative. By honoring and integrating each other's traditions, couples create a partnership that is not only grounded in respect and understanding but also vibrant with the colors of their diverse backgrounds. As partners navigate the intricate dance of merging traditions, they build a deeply rooted and endlessly evolving relationship, a testament to their love and commitment.

Retirement Planning for Couples

Retirement is often romanticized as a period of endless leisure, but it can also bring about significant shifts in relationship dynamics. The change can feel exhilarating yet daunting as you transition from structured workdays to more flexible schedules. Gone are the days dictated by alarm clocks and commutes, replaced by a blank canvas you and your partner can fill together. However, this newfound freedom can also alter roles and routines, challenging the identities you've built over decades. Please take a look at how your daily life will transform. Who will take on which household tasks? How will you balance personal time with shared activities? These questions are crucial as you navigate this significant life change.

Financial adjustments are another reality of retirement. With income sources changing from regular paychecks to savings and pensions, it's essential to reassess your financial landscape. This phase may require tightening the belt or exploring new investment opportunities. Financial planning sessions can help you understand your financial standing and make informed decisions. By setting clear retirement goals, you can align your vision for the future. Whether you dream of traveling the world, starting a new hobby, or simply enjoying the peace of home, having a shared vision ensures that both partners are moving in the same direction.

Open communication about retirement expectations is vital. It's like planning a road trip; you must agree on the destination and the route. Regular discussions about your hopes and concerns can prevent misunderstandings and ensure both partners feel heard. Consider scheduling retirement expectation discussions where you can talk candidly about your desires and fears. These conversations might touch on how you envision spending your days, your social life, or how you'll handle any health issues that arise. Keeping each other updated on financial matters is also essential. Regular financial updates can prevent surprises and help you adapt to any changes in your financial situation.

Exploring new interests can add vibrancy to your relationship post-retirement. Gone are the constraints of a 9-to-5 job, so why not delve into hobbies you've always been curious about? Whether it's painting, gardening, or joining a book club, finding activities that excite both of you can reignite passion and curiosity. Volunteering opportunities offer another avenue to stay active and engaged. Giving back to the community enriches your lives and strengthens your bond through shared purpose. Travel planning sessions can turn daydreams into plans. Imagine mapping out a trip to a place you've both longed to visit, researching the sights and experiences that await. These sessions are more than logistical; they're a chance to dream and plan together.

Joint retirement workshops are a creative way to prepare for this new chapter. These workshops provide a platform to learn about the practical aspects of retirement, from financial literacy to relationship dynamics. They offer a space to discuss common challenges and solutions with other couples, gaining insights and support. Attending these workshops together reinforces the notion that retirement is a shared experience, one where both partners can grow and adapt together.

Though a time of change, retirement offers opportunities for growth and connection. You can create a fulfilling and vibrant life together by focusing on communication, planning, and exploring new interests. As you navigate this new chapter, remember that retirement is not just an end but a beginning—a chance to redefine your relationship and discover new joys together. With the right approach, you can transform retirement into a period of enrichment and adventure, strengthening your partnership and creating lasting memories.

Chapter 10: Long-Term Relationship Growth

A ship sailing toward the horizon has a smoother journey when both captains share the same map and understand the winds guiding them. In a relationship, shared future goals help partners feel connected and in sync, like a perfect duet. This harmony brings emotional closeness, reduces conflicts, and builds teamwork. When couples work toward common dreams, they create shared meaning that deepens their understanding and unity.

To begin identifying and defining these goals, consider engaging in goal-setting workshops designed to spark conversations and uncover shared dreams. Picture a cozy evening with your favorite snacks and a stack of magazines. As you cut and paste images onto a vision board, you begin to visualize the life you aspire to build together. This creative process is more than arts and crafts; it's a tangible reflection of your shared aspirations. Future planning discussions further solidify these visions. They are the blueprints of your relationship's architecture, where you map out the milestones and steps needed to bring your goals to fruition. These discussions serve as a compass, guiding you both toward a future brimming with possibility and fulfillment.

Maintaining focus on these goals requires both diligence and creativity. Regular goal review sessions are crucial, serving as checkpoints along your journey. During these sessions, you assess your progress, celebrate victories, and adjust your sails if necessary. It's a time for reflection and recalibration, ensuring you remain on course. Additionally, consider appointing each other as accountability partners. This role isn't about playing the relationship police; instead, it's about providing gentle reminders and encouragement, supporting each other in staying committed to your shared vision. Accountability partners offer a safety net, catching each other when life's inevitable distractions threaten to steer you off track.

Achieving these joint goals brings a wealth of benefits, enriching your relationship profoundly. Working together toward a common purpose infuses your partnership with increased motivation, each step forward reinforcing your commitment to one another. It's like training for a marathon, where every mile conquered together strengthens your bond. The satisfaction derived from achieving these goals is unparalleled, fostering a sense of accomplishment and unity. As you reach each milestone, you celebrate the goal and the teamwork and cooperation that made it possible. This triumph creates a positive feedback loop, inspiring continued effort and growth and nurturing a dynamic and resilient relationship.

Vision Board Exercise

Gather your partner and a collection of magazines, scissors, and glue. Spend an evening creating a vision board, selecting images and words that represent your shared goals and dreams. Display your board in a prominent place as a daily reminder of the future you're building together, sparking conversations and inspiration along the way.

As you embark on this process of setting and achieving joint goals, remember that it's not about perfection but progress. You are co-authors of a narrative, writing a story of love, ambition, and partnership. The path may have its challenges, but with shared goals as your guide, you can navigate the journey with confidence and joy.

Continuous Learning as a Couple

In our ever-changing world, facing new challenges together is so important. Think of it as hitting the refresh button on your relationship—ensuring everything runs smoothly and is ready for whatever comes next. By prioritizing learning, both of you can truly thrive, sharing new ideas and perspectives along the way. This shared journey of exploration sparks creativity, making conversations fun and lively, and helps prevent those quiet moments that can sometimes creep into long-term relationships. So, let's celebrate this wonderful adventure of learning together—there's so much out there to discover!

Learning opportunities abound, limited only by your imagination. I would like you to consider attending workshops and seminars together. These events provide a shared experience and a springboard for discussions that can deepen your connection. Imagine the two of you at a weekend seminar, furiously taking notes, then debating the finer points over a leisurely dinner. Online courses are another fantastic resource. They allow you to explore a wide range of topics from the comfort of your home. There's a course for every interest, whether it's art history, cooking, or even astrophysics. And don't underestimate the power of a good book. Reading and discussing books together can open doors to new worlds and ideas, sparking conversations that carry on long after the final page is turned. These activities foster individual growth and strengthen your bond as you explore new concepts and insights together.

The impact of continuous learning on personal growth is profound. It broadens your perspectives, allowing you to see the world through a more nuanced lens. This expanded view can enhance problem-solving skills, providing a toolkit of strategies to navigate life's inevitable challenges. As you learn and grow, you become more adaptable and capable of handling whatever life throws your way. This adaptability is a cornerstone of a resilient relationship that can weather the storms and emerge stronger on the other side. Furthermore, learning together fosters a sense of accomplishment, reinforcing the idea that you are a team working toward common goals. It's about becoming the best versions of yourselves, individually and as a couple, continually evolving and supporting each other in the process.

To cultivate a learning mindset, consider engaging in activities that encourage curiosity and exploration. Set monthly learning goals, choosing topics that intrigue you both. These goals provide direction, ensuring that learning remains a priority. Shared learning journals are another valuable tool. Use them to record insights, reflections, and questions that arise during your educational pursuits. These journals serve as a tangible record of your growth and learning, a testament to your shared journey of discovery. Over time, they become a treasure trove of knowledge and memories, a reminder of the rich tapestry of experiences you've woven together. By prioritizing learning, you ensure that your relationship remains a source of inspiration, creativity, and growth, a dynamic partnership that thrives on curiosity and exploration.

Revisiting and Refining Relationship Skills

Relationships, much like any living entity, demand ongoing care and attention in the ever-shifting landscape of life. The concept of skill refinement in relationships might seem as elusive as finding the perfect avocado at the grocery store—ripe, yet not overdone. But just as finding that ideal avocado is worth the effort, so is continually honing the skills that make your relationship thrive. Change is a constant, and adapting to it requires more than just a positive outlook. It demands communication that isn't just heard but understood, where misinterpretations are minimized, and connections are deepened. By refining these skills, you ensure that your relationship not only survives the winds of time but flourishes.

To begin this refinement process, you could consider assessing your relationship skills with a structured approach. Self-assessment questionnaires can serve as a mirror, reflecting areas where you excel and those needing a bit more polish. These questionnaires prompt honest introspection, encouraging you to celebrate your strengths while acknowledging growth opportunities. Partner feedback sessions are equally invaluable. These sessions invite open dialogue, where both partners share insights in a supportive environment, offering constructive feedback without judgment. It's a safe space to express what's working well and what might need a slight adjustment. By engaging in these assessments, you lay the groundwork for a self-aware partnership and poised for improvement.

Once you've identified areas for enhancement, it's time to roll up your sleeves and get to work. Relationship coaching sessions provide personalized guidance, offering tailored strategies to enhance your unique dynamic. These sessions act as a sounding board, where an experienced coach helps navigate complex issues, offering fresh perspectives and tools for improvement. Skill-building workshops provide another avenue of growth. These workshops are like relationship boot camps, packed with activities designed to strengthen communication, empathy, and conflict-resolution skills. By participating in these workshops, you gain practical experience and learn new techniques that can be immediately applied to your relationship, enhancing understanding and connection.

The benefits of ongoing skill refinement are as tangible as they are rewarding. As you and your partner continue to hone your relationship skills, you'll find that challenges become less daunting. Increased confidence in handling disagreements fosters a sense of empowerment, where you approach conflicts not as adversaries but as a team. This confidence spills over into all areas of your relationship, creating a ripple effect of positivity and resilience. Greater relational harmony is another significant outcome. As communication improves and understanding deepens, you'll experience a newfound sense of peace and contentment. This harmony doesn't mean the absence of conflict but rather the presence of a shared commitment to addressing issues constructively, nurturing a stable and fulfilling partnership.

By investing in the ongoing refinement of your relationship skills, you're not just maintaining the status quo. You're actively building a foundation for a dynamic, resilient, and deeply connected partnership. Each skill refined is another thread in the tapestry of your relationship, adding richness and depth to your shared journey.

Building a Legacy of Love

Building a legacy of love is about planting seeds that will continue to grow long after you are gone, leaving a lasting impact on both your family and the broader community. It's about shared values and principles that guide your actions and decisions, creating a blueprint for those who come after you. When couples consciously work to build such a legacy, they often find that their influence extends beyond the immediate circle, touching lives and shaping the world in subtle yet profound ways. This legacy is a testament to the love and commitment shared between partners, a beacon of inspiration for children, friends, and even strangers who witness it unfolding. The values you uphold, whether it be kindness, integrity, or generosity, serve as the foundation for a legacy that transcends time, fostering a sense of continuity and purpose that binds generations together.

To create a meaningful and enduring legacy, consider engaging in activities that reflect your shared values. Volunteering can be a rewarding way to contribute to the community, offering your time and skills to causes you both care about. Whether it's mentoring youth, supporting local charities, or participating in environmental initiatives, these acts of service benefit others and strengthen your bond as a couple, reinforcing the values you hold dear. Family traditions and narratives play a significant role in legacy building, serving as the threads that weave together the tapestry of your family's history. Establish rituals and stories that celebrate your unique journey, passing them down to future generations. These traditions create a sense of belonging and identity, providing a framework for loved ones to navigate their lives with confidence and connection.

Activities like legacy vision statements and family history documentation can help clarify and articulate the legacy you wish to leave behind. A legacy vision statement is a powerful tool, capturing the essence of what you hope to achieve and leave as a couple. It serves as a guiding star, directing your actions and decisions toward a common goal. On the other hand, documenting your family history ensures that the stories and experiences that define your legacy are preserved for future generations. By capturing the past, you provide context and continuity, allowing descendants to understand their roots and draw strength from the legacy you've created. These exercises deepen your connection as a couple and reinforce the impact of your legacy on those who follow in your footsteps.

The influence of a couple's legacy on future generations is profound, shaping their values, aspirations, and sense of identity. By building a legacy of love, you inspire future family members to embrace the principles you cherished, guiding them toward lives marked by compassion, integrity, and purpose. This legacy becomes a source of pride and inspiration, a reminder of the enduring power of love and commitment. It promotes lasting values that echo through time, ensuring that the lessons and experiences you've shared continue to resonate and inspire long after you are gone. As you build this legacy, you become part of something more significant than yourselves, contributing to a continuum of love and connection that transcends the boundaries of individual lives.

Celebrating Shared Achievements

Imagine you've just completed a puzzle together, snapping the final piece into place. There's a sense of accomplishment, unity, and perhaps a bit of relief. Celebrating shared achievements in a relationship offers similar rewards. It's not just about the end result but acknowledging the teamwork that got you there. When you take time to recognize accomplishments, you reinforce the behaviors that made success possible. This acknowledgment is a powerful reminder of what you can achieve together, reinforcing your bond, much like the completed picture of that puzzle. It's a celebration of both the process and the partnership.

Recognizing milestones doesn't have to be elaborate. Simple, heartfelt gestures can be deeply meaningful. Hosting a celebration dinner offers an intimate setting to toast your success, whether it's a candlelit meal at home or a night out at your favorite restaurant. For a creative twist, consider creating an achievement scrapbook. Fill it with photos, mementos, and notes that capture the essence of your journey. Each page becomes a testament to your combined efforts and triumphs. Awarding symbolic tokens of success is another way to honor your achievements. These tokens don't have to be grand; a small keepsake inscribed with a meaningful date or phrase can serve as a lasting reminder of what you've accomplished together.

Celebrations also provide a valuable opportunity for reflection and growth. Sharing stories of the journey helps you appreciate the path you've traveled, the obstacles overcome, and the lessons learned along the way. It's a chance to laugh at the missteps, savor the victories, and acknowledge the growth that has occurred. After the celebration, consider setting new goals to keep the momentum going. Reflect on what you've learned and how to apply those insights to future endeavors. This process of reflection and goal-setting ensures that each accomplishment is not an endpoint but a stepping stone toward continued growth and success.

Celebration plays a crucial role in maintaining motivation and commitment within a relationship. You boost morale and inspire continued effort each time you recognize an achievement. It's like a shot of adrenaline, reinvigorating your partnership and reminding you of the joys of teamwork. Celebrations strengthen your commitment to one another, reinforcing the idea that together, there's little you can't achieve. As you honor your shared accomplishments, you build a reservoir of positive experiences that can be drawn upon during challenging times. These moments serve as a reminder of your resilience and capability, encouraging you to tackle future challenges with confidence and enthusiasm.

Renewing Commitment through Annual Retreats

Imagine stepping away from the daily grind, where the most pressing decision is whether to savor your morning coffee indoors or on a sun-dappled porch. Annual relationship retreats offer this precious pause, providing dedicated time for reconnection and reflection. Unlike a typical vacation, a retreat focuses on relationship growth, carving out space for relaxation and meaningful conversations often sidelined in everyday life's hustle. These retreats allow couples to step back from their routines and gain perspective, nurturing a renewed sense of partnership and clarifying their relationship vision.

Planning a retreat requires a little more thought than packing a suitcase and booking a hotel. To maximize the benefits, choose a location that holds significance or offers tranquility, such as a cozy cabin in the woods or a serene beachfront cottage. The setting should invite relaxation and foster open dialogue, free from distractions. Once you've picked the perfect spot, plan activities that strengthen your bond and open up channels of communication. Guided relationship workshops can be invaluable, offering structured exercises encouraging profound discussions. These workshops often provide new insights into each other's needs and desires, enhancing understanding and connection. In contrast, activities like nature immersion and relaxation allow you to unwind and enjoy each other's company, reinforcing the simple joy of being together.

The benefits of regular commitment renewal are profound. Retreats offer an opportunity to refresh and strengthen relationship bonds, much like a gardener tending to a beloved plant, ensuring it continues to thrive. As you focus on each other without the noise of daily obligations, you rediscover the essence of your partnership. This renewal fosters a sense of unity, reminding you of the shared journey and the love underpinning it. A clarified relationship vision often emerges, providing a roadmap for the future and aligning your goals and aspirations. This clarity shows your commitment and is a solid foundation for the road ahead.

Retreat activities should be both enjoyable and meaningful. Nature immersion, such as hiking or simply lounging by a lake, allows you to connect with the natural world and each other. These moments of tranquility create a backdrop for reflection and conversation, free from the pressures of everyday life. Guided relationship workshops offer structured time for growth, with exercises designed to deepen your understanding of each other and your relationship dynamics. Reflection and goal-setting sessions are equally crucial, encouraging you to reflect on your journey together and set intentions for the future. These activities foster a sense of purpose and direction, ensuring that your retreat is both restorative and transformative.

Chapter 10 has explored the various ways to nurture long-term relationship growth, from setting goals to celebrating achievements and renewing commitments. Each element contributes to a vibrant and resilient partnership, ready to face the challenges and joys of life together. As we move forward, consider how these practices can be woven into your relationship, creating a tapestry of love and connection that endures through time.

Review Request

Make a Difference by keeping the game alive.

"To add value to your life, simply enrich others." - Ray Vila

This book isn't just a guide; it's a lifeline for couples looking to rebuild, grow, and deepen their connection. Whether working to fix a crack in your foundation or simply wanting to strengthen your bond, LOVE WORKS has the tools to help. And now, you can help others find the same support.

How can you help?

By sharing your honest opinion of this book, you're opening the door for others to discover what could make a real difference in their lives. Many people are just like you—searching for answers, hope, and guidance. Your review could be the reason someone takes that first step toward improving their relationship.

It's easy, free, and takes less than a minute. And your review could:

- Show couples they're not alone.
- Help them find tools to rebuild trust and intimacy.
- Give them hope for a brighter future together.

Want to make an impact?

Just scan the QR code below or visit this link to leave your review:

https://www.amazon.com/review/review-your-purchases/?asin=B0DWL1HJG6

Thank you for being part of this mission to help couples everywhere. Every review keeps the potential for healing and connection alive. Together, we can make a difference—one relationship at a time.

With gratitude,
Ray Vila

Conclusion

As we reach the last page of this workbook, let's take a moment to reflect on the journey we've taken together! Throughout this book, we've explored the wonderful world of relationships, focusing on essential topics like communication, resolving conflicts, enhancing intimacy, and navigating life's changes. We've also talked about building emotional intelligence, embracing vulnerability, and finding ways to add excitement to our everyday lives. Plus, we've emphasized the value of spending quality time together, celebrating our differences, and laying the groundwork for lasting growth. It's been quite the adventure!

The core of what we've learned centers around the power of open communication and empathy. Remember, speaking from the heart and genuinely listening to your partner can transform misunderstandings into opportunities for deeper connection. Regular check-ins become the lifeline of your relationship, ensuring that you're always in tune with one another's needs and desires. Growth doesn't stop with this book; it's an ongoing journey. The tools and strategies we've discussed serve as a foundation for continuous development, helping you weave a rich tapestry of love and understanding.

Celebrate the progress you've made. You've shown dedication and courage by diving into this workbook. Recognize the positive changes you've witnessed in your relationship, no matter how small they may seem. Each step forward is a triumph worthy of celebration. Your commitment to nurturing your relationship is commendable, and I hope you feel the pride you so deserve.

But the journey doesn't end here. I would like you to continue applying the skills and strategies you've learned. Use them as a compass guiding you through the ever-evolving landscape of your relationship. Remember, growth is a process, not a destination. Embrace the challenges and triumphs ahead with an open heart and a flexible mindset. Adapt these strategies to fit your unique circumstances. After all, every relationship is a distinct blend of personalities, histories, and dreams.

I encourage you to revisit sections of this book that resonate with your current challenges. You can use it as an ongoing resource. The exercises and practices are designed to be revisited and refined as you grow together. Consider this book a supportive companion on your journey, always ready to offer guidance and inspiration.

I want to express my heartfelt gratitude to each of you. Your commitment to strengthening your relationship is a true testament to the love and dedication you share. Remember, transformation is achievable with patience and effort. Believe in the strength of your connection and the power of your partnership.

As you reflect on your journey through this workbook, consider sharing your experiences with others. Your insights could serve as a beacon of hope and inspiration for couples on a similar path. I invite your feedback not only to celebrate your successes but also to learn how this book has impacted your relationship.

As we conclude, I want to leave you with a heartfelt sentiment: Love truly flourishes when we come together as partners. Much like a garden, relationships need our caring hands, attentive hearts, and a sprinkle of light to thrive. Picture it as a delicate cake, where each layer needs to be added thoughtfully to create something beautiful and meaningful. You're fostering a vibrant and enduring connection by nurturing your bond with love and the wisdom you've gathered. Remember to keep nurturing each other and embrace the beauty of your shared journey, for every step you take together is just as valuable as the destination you're reaching for.

References

- *What Are the 5 Love Languages? Definition and Examples*
  https://www.psychologytoday.com/us/blog/click-here-happiness/202009/what-are-the-5-love-languages-definition-and-examples

- *5 Steps to Gottman Active Listening [Tips from a Couples ...*
  https://www.lisachentherapy.com/blog/5-steps-to-gottman-active-listening-tips-from-a-couples-therapist

- *Communicating Mindfully in Relationships*
  https://www.psychologytoday.com/us/blog/conscious-communication/201709/communicating-mindfully-in-relationships

- *How to Express Your Needs without Feeling Needy*
  https://amiethedatingcoach.com/how-to-express-your-needs-without-feeling-needy/#:~:text=When%20you%20express%20your%20needs,developing%20solutions%20rather%20than%20complaints.

- *Conflict Resolution in Relationships & Couples: 5 Strategies* https://positivepsychology.com/conflict-res

olution-relationships/

- *The Value of Role Play in Couples Therapy in Pasadena, CA* https://californiaintegrativetherapy.com/the-value-of-role-plays-in-couples-therapy-a-journey-of-experiential-healing/#:~:text=Role%20plays%20serve%20as%20a,resolution%2C%20and%20emotional%20regulation%20skills.

- *Constructive Criticism in a Relationship: Importance & Tips* https://www.marriage.com/advice/relationship/constructive-criticism-in-relationships/

- *How to Set Boundaries in Your Relationships* https://psychcentral.com/relationships/why-healthy-relationships-always-have-boundaries

- *Daily Rituals of Connection* https://www.gottman.com/blog/3-daily-rituals-that-stop-spouses-from-taking-each-other-for-granted/

- *The Power of Touch: Physical Affection is Important ... - IU Blogs* https://blogs.iu.edu/kinseyinstitute/2020/05/28/the-power-of-touch-physical-affection-is-important-in-relationships-but-some-people-need-more-than-others/

- *45 Hobbies for Couples to Strengthen Your Bond* https://www.purewow.com/wellness/hobbies-for-couples

- *10 Ways To Create A Romantic Atmosphere At Home* https://shabbyfufu.com/10-ways-to-create-a-romantic-atmosphere-at-home/

- *When Couples Become Parents: The Impact on Your ...* https://www.psychologytoday.com/us/blog/preparing-for-parenthood/202303/when-couples-become-parents-the-impact-on-your-relationship
- *Positive Coparenting Strategies | USU* https://extension.usu.edu/relationships/faq/positive-coparenting-strategies
- *How Dual-Career Couples Make It Work* https://hbr.org/2019/09/how-dual-career-couples-make-it-work
- *How To Effectively Navigate Life Transitions As A Couple* https://www.thecounsellingplace.com/blog/how-to-effectively-navigate-life-transitions-as-a-couple#:~:text=Building%20resilience%20as%20a%20team&text=Open%20communication%3A%20Create%20a%20safe,perspective%20and%20validate%20their%20feelings.&text=Set%20mutual%20goals%3A%20Identify%20shared%20goals%20and%20priorities%20as%20a%20couple.
- *Understanding Emotional Triggers and Building Healthy ...* https://www.sunshinecitycounseling.com/blog/emotional-triggers-and-relationship-issues-in-therapy#:~:text=These%20triggers%20can%20stem%20from,criticism%2C%20betrayal%2C%20and%20loss.
- *Strengthening Emotional Resilience in Relationships* https://www.marriagefamilyservices.com/post/strengthening-emaotional-resilience-in-relationships/
- *Empathy In Marriage: The Secret To Thriving Relationships* https://www.sdrelationshipplace.com/empathy

-in-marriage-secret-to-thriving-relationships/

- *Feelings Check-In - What is an emotional check-in?* https://empoweredtherapy.org/feelings-check-in-emotional-check-in-7-questions-to-ask-yourself-today/#:~:text=You%20can%20start%20by%20asking,and%20offer%20support%20without%20judgment.

- *The Importance of Vulnerability in Healthy Relationships* https://www.psychologytoday.com/us/blog/happy-healthy-relationships/202203/the-importance-of-vulnerability-in-healthy-relationships

- *Understanding How Childhood Experiences Shape Adult ...* https://www.thecounsellingplace.com/blog/understanding-how-childhood-experiences-shape-adult-intimacy-issues-by-lim-swee-chen#:~:text=Witnessing%20frequent%20conflict%20or%20experiencing,difficulties%20in%20forming%20secure%20bonds.

- *7 Ways to Create Emotional Safety in Your Relationship* https://psychcentral.com/blog/how-do-you-create-emotional-safety-in-your-relationships

- *Couples Therapy Case Study: Anna and Brian* https://www.ebtc.ie/case-examples-3/couplestherapyhelped/

- *Spontaneity and Intimacy: Should You Let It All Hang Out?* https://www.psychologytoday.com/us/blog/my-side-of-the-couch/202304/spontaneity-and-intimacy-should-you-let-it-all-hang-out

- *The Role of Shared Hobbies and Interests in Relationships* https://vocal.media/psyche/the-role-of-shared-hobbies-and-interests-in-relationships
- *4 Reasons Why Traveling Strengthens Your Relationship* https://www.followyourdetour.com/reasons-why-traveling-strengthens-your-relationship/
- *15 Relationship Milestones That Are Worth Celebrating* https://www.marriage.com/advice/relationship/relationship-milestones-that-are-worth-celebrating/
- *31 Simple Time Management Hacks for Married Couples* https://www.modernhusbands.com/post/31-simple-time-management-hacks-for-married-couples
- *The Power of Relationship Check-Ins - Irina Baechle* https://www.irinabaechlecounselingllc.com/irina-baechle-counseling/the-power-of-relationship-check-ins#:~:text=What%20are%20the%20Benefits%20of,in%20of ive%20to%20thirty%20minutes.
- *Digital Detox For Couples* https://lindseyhoskins.com/digital-detox-for-couples/
- *Why Scheduling Sex Can Be Important For Your Marriage* https://jillsavage.org/why-scheduling-sex-can-be-important-for-your-marriage/
- *Cultural Impact on Modern Relationships: A Deep Dive* https://startmywellness.com/2024/06/cultural-differences-shape-relationships/
- *Navigating Different Values in A Relationship* https://coupleslearn.com/different-values-in-a-relationship/

- *Effective Communication in Inclusive Relationships* https://improvinglivescounseling.com/effective-communication-in-inclusive-relationships-bridging-differences-with-grace/

- *Cultural Impact on Modern Relationships: A Deep Dive* https://startmywellness.com/2024/06/cultural-differences-shape-relationships/

- *How Shared Goals Can Strengthen Your Relationship* https://www.laureltherapy.net/blog/how-shared-goals-can-strengthen-your-relationship#:~:text=Setting%20goals%20in%20a%20relationship%20is%20like%20having%20a%20roadmap,it%20enhances%20their%20emotional%20intimacy.

- *The Benefits of Continuous Learning* https://trainual.com/manual/continuous-learning

- *Healthy Communication Tips - Relationships* https://www.verywellmind.com/managing-conflict-in-relationships-communication-tips-3144967

- *The Ultimate DIY Guide to Planning a Gottman Couples ...* https://laurasilverstein.co/couples-retreat-gottman-method/